Interpreting Lilith

Delphine Gloria Jay

Copyright 1981 by Delphine Jay
All rights reserved.

No part of this book may be reproduced or transmitted in any form or by any means, electronic or mechanical, including photocopying or recording, or by any information storage and retrieval system, without written permission from the author and publisher. Request d inquiries may be mailed to American Federation of Astrologers, Inc., 6535 S. Rural Rd., Tempe, AZ 85283.

First Printing 1981
Fifth Printing 2010

ISBN-10: 0-86690-264-3
ISBN-13: 978-0-86690-264-9

LCC: 83-72650

Cover Design: Jack Cipolla

Published by:
American Federation of Astrologers, Inc.
6535 S. Rural Road
Tempe, AZ 85283

www.astrologers.com

Printed in the United States of America

Dedication

This book is dedicated to my dear husband Gene,
with gratitude for his support and inspiration.

Contents

Introduction	xi
Chapter One, Astronomical History and Legends	1
Chapter Two, The Lilith Influence	9
Chapter Three, Lilith Through the Signs	25
Chapter Four, Lilith Through the Houses	53
Chapter Five, Aspects to Lilith	97
Chapter Six, Lilith in Return Charts	119

Foreword

There are two different types of astrology books on the market today. The more popular type is written to re-explain ideas others have put forth, or ideas passed down from antiquity. The author's purpose in those books is to try to explain in more modern and/or personal terms the language of astrology. I include in this category books that simply expound personal views on areas or subjects in which the authors have put forth opinions. The second type of book is much rarer, for in that category is presented the basic research that expands astrology in new directions. There are very few books on validated basic research presented, because the labor to do this type of work is so difficult and involved. Few researchers are also good authors, in the sense that they are willing to take time from their first love (research) to document for the general public the different effects they have found. The reader of this book will be quite fortunate to have found not only a book that is the result of good basic research but one from a person whom I consider to be one of the very finest researchers in astrology today.

Delphine Jay has worked to try to determine the effects of Lilith for many years. This book is the result of her efforts, and it fills a need for a more completely documented and researched view of Lilith. In it you will find described the effects of Lilith that she has discovered. Her purpose in presenting this information at this time is simply that her work has reached a point where it can be presented. It is by no means finished, as no research work is ever finished, but it is in final enough form that good and useful material is ready to be presented to you for your reading and further retesting.

Dr. Zipporah Dobyns prefaces all of her work with the advice that what is being presented is a theory to be tested; that nothing which is being presented is so factually true that it should be accepted as truth without further personal validation by the reader or user. So it is with the research on Lilith that Delphine presents in this book. What makes it easier on the reader, though, is the fine form in which her research is presented. This is a very important feature of the book. Ms. Jay gives enough material on the effects of Lilith so that readers can immediately test or apply her work in their astrological practice.

When Delphine first presented me with the work she was doing on Lilith, I was quite skeptical that such an effect could exist. First of all, I thought if it were so important, why hadn't others written about it? Next, I thought, why hadn't the astronomers discovered this body? Much to my surprise I was to learn that, unlike many of the other hypothetical (i.e., undiscovered) planets, not only had very many good astrologers written on the effects of Lilith but astronomers have for years been playing with the elusive body that asserts to be the Lilith that Delphine describes.

Having discovered that, then, the only thing lingering after my original argument was the question of why I had not personally tried to see if it really worked in the way that astrologers described that it would. I did try, and it did work—and I became a convert to its effects. Since that time I have tried Lilith in many different ways, and have found that it consistently works, and in the way it had been described that it should work!

It is now time to tell others of the importance of this work. This is an important book! It should be read and used by all astrologers everywhere. It is with this hope that this book is presented. May your efforts to work in this area be rewarded with new insight!

Michael P. Munkasey
March 20, 1980

Foreword

This is undoubtedly the most comprehensive and complete book on Lilith that has been published anywhere to date. Many years of personal research went into the writing of this book. Jay starts from Lilith's astronomical history and legends. She goes on to give some very comprehensive delineations of Lilith through each sign, house and aspect, based upon her own personal observations. The last chapter covers the delineation of Lilith in Return Charting by house position. While the author claims that no book can be the last word on Lilith, it is certainly in my own opinion the most comprehensive and complete work on Lilith we have today.

Robert Carl Jansky
April 1981

Hug then thy dream,
Poor fool! I am no dream, who offer thee
Rapture and peace at cost of sterile pride.

Thou dost deny and question, but mine eyes
Gleam on thee, being lit with alien light;
My lips proclaim thee mysteries; mine arms
Are bond for all thy doubts, not mist nor mud,
But all that gods desire and fools reject:
Behold me!

My name thou knowest not, and yet shalt know,
And know too late. But know thou this indeed:
Joy is my sister, sister I to Death.

He conquers me
Who dares to pay my price. My price thou know'st.

Excerpts from the lyric play LILITH, written by George Sterling in 1919 and published by The MacMillan Company, New York 1926.

Introduction

This book is written as an attempt to put into workable perspective the unique astrological point given the name Lilith. As a shadowy globe, Lilith has been known to astrology since the early 1700s, but remains elusive enough in motion to escape the precise daily detection that is understandably necessary to prove its existence as a satellite, particularly to closed minds.

This book contains the essence of my findings to date concerning the influence of Lilith in the natal chart. Conclusions from personal research are shared with those of you who, in turn, share my curiosity, in the hope that you are assisted in taking these observations further.

I am grateful for the pertinent insights regarding Lilith that have been reported over the years. They have immeasurably aided my investigations that began, naturally enough, in curiosity and quickly grew into serious study. After more than eight years, I could no longer deny viable influence and provocative action attributable to Lilith in natal charts.

In this small effort I will not attempt, at length, to qualify the existence astronomically, since this is being dealt with elsewhere by others. However, documented European sightings from which the Lilith ephemerides are compiled are listed in Chapter One, beginning with the first such sighting by astronomer Riccioli who report the crossing of the dark globe over the Sun on September 2, 1618; pertinent information on its orbit; technical data gathered from these observations; and the long history of legends concerning Lilith to date. Instead, the work is designed to interest those who share with me the desire to test Lilith in the practical manner, leaving the final debate to the findings we must consistently verify.

With substantial knowledge of, and respect for, the astrological root principles, we can deal responsibly and safely with particular areas. As of this printing, Lilith's daily positions are given by its mean motion in the Lilith ephemerides, due to our not having the exact time of day when the conjunctions of Lilith and the Sun occurred in the reports. Therefore, a leeway of one degree is necessary to keep in mind when delineating Lilith in a chart, particularly when cusping a sign or house. For this reason, in these test efforts, we keep orbs small: five for aspects to the planets and six for the Sun and Moon are sufficiently safe as an average. However, consider the slightly wider orb when another planet or planets are involved through association.

Though the precise daily exactitudes are still to be revealed in its apparent orbit around the Earth as a nonreflective satellite or dark moon, this is insufficient reason to ignore Lilith's existence totally. This is paraticularly true as the list of qualified astrologers who have tested Lilith over the years and agree to its definite influence has grown considerably.

Although the negative influence of Lilith's effect in human behavior has been soundly established, we know that where there is a negative there is logically a positive, which challenged my sense of proportions for this research. Read with creative awareness in mind, and you may well uncover a wealth of insight revealed by Lilith's house position and sign in the horoscope you study. Evidence is consistently being accumulated regarding the key behavior patterns that Lilith underlies. I share with you in the following pages some of this evidence for your consideration and evaluation.

Delphine Jay
April 1978

Chapter 1

Astronomical History and Legends

A great deal has been shared through the years about the legends that surround Lilith and the long history of Lilith investigations, with insights and conclusions reported by astrologers since 1918, when Sepharial first brought Lilith to attention. Without those early and inspired pioneering efforts, which at first provoked curiosity and then interest, we could not have come as far as we have in our knowledge of the natural maturing process on the mundane-emotional level that Lilith represents. Lilith provides inspiration in the otherwise impersonal levels of the mind and the creative spirit we all long to express. For those who have not yet investigated Lilith, it will prove to be a fascinating study of extremes in influence that will open the natal chart to greater humanistic understanding.

I give special thanks to Ivy Goldstein Jacobson, without whose Lilith ephemeris my research efforts could not have begun. Until greater exactitude could be computed, this ephemeris served as the mean standard. It proved very reliable, if orbs were kept sufficiently tight. One half those of the Moon are suggested.

The orbit of Lilith is tabulated from one conjunction of the Sun to the next conjunction. Apparently a nonreflective body, Lilith had been observed by European astronomers long before the discovery of Pluto, at approximate six-month intervals, as a black or dark body crossing over the Sun, or as a fiery globe when opposite the Sun. However, the exact time of day when these sightings were made had not always been reported in the record, making necessary the approximation of its mean daily motion. This was set at 3o. Since then it has been more closely defined as ranging from three degrees to 3°2' per day. The ephemeris in Jacobson's book, *The Dark Moon Lilith in Astrology,* was the forerunner for the monthly positions used in earliest research. Daton, in her book, *Lilith,* later provided us with positions for every ten days, with further refinements in the adjustment for leap years, giving us another valuable step forward in exactitude.

Bearing in mind the basic principles of the signs and houses, the result has been great accuracy for chart interpretation, verified by transits. Using symbolic directions these positions have also been found to be valuable in determining future trends. Allow one-half degree applying and separating when directing Lilith because of the minutes in variation of correctness, due to the positions at standard mean motion.

Hopefully, one day, through more sophisticated tracking equipment, or as a result of space travel using higher orbits, the components of Lilith's travel around Earth will be soundly established. Until then, and bearing in mind the variables in daily motion, this book focuses on conclusions verified from personal research and insights into of behavioral patterns of Lilith. They are primarily found by sign and house positions, and secondarily by aspect.

Lilith has been an astrological curiosity for more than a century, and a mythological one since the time of Adam. Lilith has stubbornly resisted being disproved, remaining in the annals of astrology, almost as a nuisance. Over the years Lilith has successfully attracted esoterically inspired astrological researchers who have not suffered from the overly scientific approach that negates creative imagination. They have discovered substantial patterns of behavior that Lilith consistently explains in the horoscope.

Early Discoveries
Lilith was first named by Sepharial, an outstanding researcher on Lilith. He first introduced Lilith in his book, *The Science of Foreknowledge,* written circa 1918. The chapter entitled "The New Satellite Lilith" opened this fascinating new ground to astrologers with his report on its sighting January 1, 1898, at 215° longitude or 5 Scorpio. The sighting was officially documented by German astronomer Dr. Georges Waltemath of Hamburg on January 22, 1898, in which the location of the orbit of the second satellite of the Earth was given. It was published in *The Globe* on Febrary 7 of that year. Sepharial opened this new ground with his conclusions as to the manner in which to begin compiling an approximate ephemeris from which we have since begun observations of Lilith in natal charts. The sightings were primarily made on the dates when the dark body transited over the solar face. The observed dates given were: June 6, 1761; November 19, 1762; May 3, 1764; June 11, 1855; and October 24, 1881. Lilith's synodical period was set at 177 days. Lilith's cycle is 126 years, the lesser cycle being 63 years. Lilith orbits

the Earth every 119 days, or approximately ten days per zodiacal sign, which, in my transit research, has proved valid.

Sepharial calculated dates when the Sun and Lilith would be in the same geocentric longitude from 1854 to 1901; they proved correct to within several days of official sightings that were reported February 16, 1897, at Stuttgart and Munchen. They coincided with the conjunctions that were calculated by Dr. Waite for early February and the end of July 1898. The tables used by Sepharial were published in *The Science of Foreknowledge*.

In astronomy, knowledge of the satellite, later to be named Lilith, dates to September 2, 1618, when Italian astronomer Riccioli reported observation of the dark body in its approach to opposition, recorded in *Almagestum Novum,* Volume ii, p. 16. On November 7, 1700, it was sighted at Montpellier by Maraldi and Cassini, and recorded in 1701 in *Memoires de l'Academie* in France.

The following are later-recorded dates of observations of Lilith conjunctions and oppositions to the Sun. These sightings were primarily made when the dark body transited the solar face or was traveling at or near opposition.

- December 23, 1719, in Hungary, five days before opposition.
- March 27, 1720, and March 15, 1721, at Fauer by Dr. Allischer.
- June 29, 1735, by the Rev. Ziegler at Gotha, Germany, three days prior to opposition. The information and a painted impression was published by Ziegler.
- June 6, 1761, at St. Neots, Huntingdonshire, and published in *The London Chronicle*. The same day also reported by Scheuten at Onfeld.
- November 19, 1762, by Lichtenberg and Sollnitz near Erlangen, Germany.
- May 3, 1764, near Gotha, Germany, by Hoffman.
- March 25, 1784, by Superintendent Fritzsch, at Quedlinburg, Germany, and reported in *Bode's Astron, Alk.* in 1805.
- January 16, 1818, by Capel Lofft at Ipswich, Great Britain.
- October 20, 1839, in Rome by Decuppis.
- June 11, 1855, by Dr. Ritter of Hanover, Germany. Spotted near Naples, the round black body was seen crossing the Sun's disc from west to east.
- September 4, 1879, by Gowey at North Lewisburg, Ohio. Recorded in *Monthly Weather Review of the United States* (U.S. Weather Bureau, Washington, D.C.).
- February 16, 1897, at Munich and at Stuttgart, Germany, from 8:45 a.m. until 12:45 p.m.
- February 4, 1898, at Wiesbaden, Germany, at 8:15 a.m. by Dr. Georges Waltemath, and a second time at Griefwald at 1:30 a.m. by Ziegler, again as one in a group of no fewer than twelve observers.

Most of the observers described Lilith as a round black or dark body when seen at conjunction with the Sun, and as a reddish or fiery globe in its approach to opposition of the Sun. Based upon Berlin Local Mean Time, the elements of the new satellite given by Dr. Waltemath were:

- Approximate daily motion: 3 degrees
- Synodic revolution: 177 days
- Equatorial radius of the Earth in distance: 161 radii, 700 kilometers (or approximately 435 miles) in diameter
- Lilith is 1/80th in mass as compared with the Earth. It is almost three times as far from Earth as our Moon, but only one-quarter the size of the Moon and moving only one-quarter as quickly

The seriousness with which Sepharial supported the existence of yet a second Earth moon cannot be taken lightly. He also anticipated a new planet would be found beyond Neptune—one that would be essentially martial in nature, but infinitely more powerful, even to its probable name, "Pluto." Until this coup in the astronomical world occured, there had been continual study of Lilith, particularly in Ultrecht, Holland, where a special bureau had been established solely for its observation. A third satellite, or Earth moon, was also observed at that time by Dr. Waltemath; however, not as much was known of its elements as was known of Lilith. Reference to the aforementioned work is suggested for those who are interested in knowing more about this third moon.

The determinations of Lilith's motions were originally calculated not only by Sepharial, for whose pioneering dynamics and incredible insight we are greatly indebted, but also by Genty, whose list of sightings was published in 1925 in the *Viole d'sis,* and by Marcel Gama, Tamos, and Tisserand, the latter contributing to the collation of the dates of observations. From 1870 to 1923, the prestigious publishers of Raphael's ephemerides, W. Foulsham & Co., Ltd., London, published ephemerides not only for Lilith but for the third satellite also, offering the zodiacal determinations of both.

Ivy Jacobson's source of information was the official paper by German astronomers, listing Lilith positions between 1870 and 1936, with special adjustments made that were required because of the discrepency caused by February's variation in days, together with the additional variability caused by the satellite's erratic seconds of motion and the irregular waiting period for the next sighting. The positions were determined before 1870 back to 1860. The positions after 1936 were projected to the year 2000, with consideration made for Lilith's otherwise regular return in 63 years—the lesser cycle (the cycle being 126 years).

Without the findings of the past, the subject might still remain in limbo, having been transcended in awareness by the discovery of Pluto in 1930. That major breakthrough in astronomy abruptly switched European observations of Lilith to the awesome potential of the intriguing new trans-Neptunian planet. However, in recent times, reports on the continued observation of the dark satellite orbiting the Earth by Soviet scientist Yuri Pskovsky, master of physics and mathematics and senior research associate at the Shternberg State Astronomy Institute have been published in the *Moscow News* (1966), a Russian daily printed in the English language.

Pskovsky was asked to comment on the earlier press reports of observations carried out by U.S. astronomers on two natural satellites of the Earth other than the Moon—both satellites being reported as clouds of dust traveling along the Moon's orbit. Said Pskovsky, "Soviet scientists and their colleagues abroad keep a constant watch on the dust satellites of the Earth. They were (according to the Russians) discovered in 1961-1962 by Professor Kazmierz Kordylewski, a Polish astronomer. It is exceedingly difficult to observe them with a conventional telescope. They can be observed only on moonless nights, and then only when they are in a position directly opposite the Sun and nowhere near the Milky Way. Naturally, such convenient conditions do not come about often (enough)." Sepharial said, "A conjunction of Lilith and the Sun does not infer a visible transit of the Sun's disc. It will depend upon the position of the satellite in its orbit at the time, and the inclination of the orbit to the plane of the ecliptic."

The report goes on to say that knowledge of a dust cloud within which the Earth itself is engulfed was known by astronomers long ago. The *Moscow News* reported that "V. Moroz, a Soviet scientist, recently proved that the density of this cloud is gradually increasing. He assumes that the Earth adds, by its gravitational pull, some 300-400 million tons of cosmic dust to this cloud every year. A small part of it—about a million tons—falls out annually onto the surface of our planet."

"This dust is also the material from which the new natural satellites of the Earth are formed. Just like the Moon, they have phases, their brightness changing with their position in relation to the sun and the observer on the earth," says Pskovsky. "These natural Earth satellites are outside the orbits followed so far by space vehicles. But there is no doubt that as interplanetary travel progresses these orbits will change." It is surmised that, as we develop more sophisticated orbits, more will be known of these natural sisters of the Moon.

In 1969 an English publication, *The New Scientist,* reported on the findings of American scientist Dr. John Bagby, who stated that "Several natural satellites circle Earth in calculated orbits." Two of the satellites were later photographed in their projected travel from his calculations. Several decades before the turn of the century, the United States Weather Bureau had officially recognized Lilith as an asteroid or minor planet. However, that seemed to be as far as it went. In all reports it is consistently referred to as a "cloud or dustlike body" seen only against the backdrop of the Sun. How fitting the name "Lilith," which means dust-cloud, for the first of these sister Moons. Another of its legendary names is "Owl"—the night bird that remains in the shadows—much as the influence of Lilith remains in the shadows of human nature beyond the emotional stimuli of our first moon.

In the lyric drama *Lilith* based on his dramatic poem, George Sterling pictures Lilith, in the words of Theodore Dreiser,[1] "As extracting joy from the (emotional) suffering of another. On the other hand, she is the cause of an intense joy that sets itself against pain as its equivalent—its fair exchange and reward." He speaks of "this precious flower of consciousness" saying, "if life can produce a thought form such as this (Lilith)—then it is not so unendurable, be its darker phases what they may." Sterling claimed the poem to be symbolic of the illusions of love and idealism, depicting the contrast between pain and pleasure and "that strangest and most awful of human faculties—our ability to be happy when we know others are in agony." How deftly he pictured the lowest strains in the human makeup (Lilith at the lower point), as against the beauty and love we are intellectually and spiritually capable of (Lilith at the higher point).

Legends
Lilith, the derivative of the word *laylah* in Hebraic, means "night," befitting the darkness in which the satellite so named orbits, and the night, or dark side of the desire nature in humans, with which it identifies. Lilith, rich in Semitic tradition and Jewish demonology, was fabled as the woman of pre-Adamic race who was Adam's twin sister and first wife, who refusing to bear his issue instead bore of Samael, the fallen angel, three demons, and called the Lilim. She was "fabled" as the demonic queen who seduced Adam; as the spirit of evil through her demonic offspring who fill the world, from which infants must be ceremonially cleansed by traditional Jewish rites; as a vampirizer of infants, in which spirit we might also consider Lilith in connection with crib deaths, child abuse, and back-street abortions; and the seductive temptress of men who sleep alone. In connection to the last mentioned, Lilith is often found as the other woman, office wife or the prostitute. Lilith is also fabled as one who seeks to slay men in their desires. Is it an Adamic male-superiority syndrome that Lilith seeks to slay in human nature through the inspiration of feminine activism? You might say that we have found our little black sheep in the solar family—black, meaning, in the author's opinion, dark to the material understanding or the lower dance in life. Lilith is not of Ceasar's world. Thus, giving unto it here; in other words, to be selfishly motivated (self-oriented) within the rulerships of its position is, from empirical evidence classically negative in effect, decidedly malefic.

Aramaic, Oriental, and Yiddish amulets protect women in childbirth from the (so-called) evil powers of Lilith, were popularly worn, or placed over the bed, to guarantee safe births. The early Hebraic version contained not only the names of the three angels that were divinely sent to influence Lilith's return from degeneracy, but also their likenesses (Alphabet of Ben Sira),

---
[1] Famous American Novelist (1871-1945), known for his unsparing and poignant realism. Author of *An American Tragedy*.

which had been made through the 1700s. The Orientals depicted an amulet of the Lilith spirit as being bound by chains. In ancient times it was said that Lilith favored children born out of wedlock who, when smiling in their sleep, indicated her being close and keeping special watch over them—alluding to the phrase of "devouring them."

In Blavatsky's *The Secret Doctrine,* mindless Liliths were said to be the progeny of the spiritually inspired third and fourth races who interbred with the "daughters of men"—still in the human-animal passional stages of development. In this manner, bred into the lower consciousness of the race, where it is alien, Lilith was malefic to the lower desire nature such progeny supposedly carried. Thus, the fables that followed of Lilith's begotten strain of demons were said to translate themselves into human behavior as mindlessly treacherous and emotionally sadistic. This was understandable. Also called the "Screeching Night Bird," Lilith exemplifies the human condition in its night, or dark stages, of universal consciousness. Lilith is indicative of the idea of one's hand being slapped, or desires denied, if you will, when consciousness is directed downward, automatically altering such vacuum or abruptly realizing its evil to the native's awareness. Lilith, as the primal factor in man's link to a pre-Adamic existence, appears to be the subjective instinctive link to the creative factor of the mind and spirit. As such, on lower levels, where it is denied (emotional-material), it is a disturbing influence.

Legends of the Lilith-type woman, and first wife of Adam, precede the Jewish literature of biblical times by many centuries. In Hindu scriptures the Puranas tell of the Chhaya form (ancient) of begetting life, a primeval method of birth by asexual propagation. We find such allusions to Lilith in the oft mentioned stories of the Sun's marriage to the unfeeling daughter of Vishvakarman, who leaves him with only her Chhaya shadow, or astral image, which he mistakes for her, and by whom the first children were said to be begotten. Having fled into the night, she is said to have consecrated herself thereafter to religious service. Later in the stories of the sage Kandu is beguiled by the poignantly beautiful nymph Pramlocha who was sent by the inferior desire gods to prostitute him. Upon his banishment of her, after a period of hypnotic reveries, she begat a lovely woman-child. These are scriptural references to cycles of evolution when the original race to inhabit the Earth said to be exalted beings in etherically corporealized bodies that parented the first stages of humanity. The ancient shadow of this exaltation alludes to the remarkable creative talent and deep sense of devotion that can be unearthed where Lilith is in the chart. However, this is only when the native has sufficiently overcome his or her lower desires in the house and the sign of Lilith.

Legends of the sixteenth century refer to the Lilith spirit as a lovely woman of "cat-like" form. In the middle ages Lilith was referred to as a wind bird that flies alone at night wailing. Both the cat and the owl, with their arresting eyes and composure, have always exemplified a strange kind of wisdom or knowledge. It is almost like a form of repose that is difficult to be at ease with. So it is with Lilith types who seek to want to "know" you, with eyes that appear as if coming from a distant place. Like the brilliance of Scorpio eyes, they can be masked, only to flash momentarily. The difference between the two is that whereas the former are intensely searching, the latter has found it, which to some is unsettling and to those who do not understand, flirtatious—the modern word for beguiling or bewitching.

To the ancient Chaldeans, Lilith was known as "Lilatu." The Assyrians called it "Lay'la," and the Semitic tribes, "Alitat." The old Jewish Talmud refers to it as "Adam's first wife," "queen of evil," and the "mother of demons." Lilith has been likened to Kali, the Hindu goddess, and to the aspect of Siva that is effective in matters of intrigue and treachery.

The fixed star of Algol at 25 Taurus, representing the head of the Gorgon Medusa, was known as Lilith by the Hebrews—after the nocturnal vampire said to be Adam's first wife. The Medusa was one of three Gorgon sisters. She was the only sister who was mortal and was, originally a beautiful maiden. However, as a consequence of becoming the mother of Pegasus and Chrysaor by Neptune in one of Minerva's temples, Minerva transformed her hair into a head of hissing serpents. So fearful was the sight of her, that those who looked upon her were said to have been turned instantly to stone.

By way of the legends of Lilith, studied by students of the Talmud, the word found its way into scriptures—in Isaiah 34:14 as the "screech owl" in the King James version; and as a "night monster" in the Revised Edition. References to the Lilith influence upon the minds of men appear again and again, because the realization that something, thus far not yet fully explored, exists and affects human behavior in our surrounding heavenly bodies, and must be dealt with to more fully understand the human factor.

Chapter Two

The Lilith Influence

The following observations are based on Lilith's apparent orbit of the Earth as our second satellite. Representing yet a further moon, Lilith indicates still another level of human consciousness that is representative of a dimmer (less reflective) past than that which is symbolized by Luna. Sepharial says, "The idea is not preposterous when taken with the concept of reincarnation, since such no-longer luminous bodies still persevere in their old paths, and even the Moon, although luminous, is little more in itself than an old and abandoned limekiln." He further says, "Esotericists seem to require the existence of such bodies in their concept of the Earth Chain—bodies which may be regarded as the grandmothers and great-grandmothers of our globe, as the Moon is its mother, the former habitation of Earth's humanity."

As we know, the bright Moon Luna represents our immediate subconscious storehouse of *personal* memory, through which our conscious awareness is instinctively prompted through feeling. As our basic lunar channel, it, by sign, makes available to us the instinctive feelings that make up our emotional Desire Nature, and thus our emotional makeup. In other words, the obvious subjective personality that is *immediately* reactive to one's environment. From this we conclude that the Moon Luna rules the emotional soul. With this in mind, it is both logical and reasonable that Lilith as another apparent instinct phenomenon (lunar trait), which in remaining dark and thus non-reflective (or deeper in our psyche), holds in abeyance on emotional levels, or essentially limits the essence of a deeper mind flow. Ruling the more sophisticated creative desire nature, Lilith appears to be a mode of transmission for the awakening and impersonalizing influence of Uranus (upper octave of Mercury) and for the transformational ray of Pluto (upper octave of the Moon). Lilith thus produces sudden compulsive changes (as the interaction of these two planets describe), the effect of which is dependent on one's ability to successfully depersonalize. As the Moon personalizes, Lilith *de*personalizes. The result is a certain amount of sophisticated awareness.

We attribute to Luna the subconscious emotional processes, instinctive or *sub*jective feelings, and the channel through which mediumistic perceptions flow. We may probe the subconcious process more deeply for Lilith to tap the instinctive *reasoning* processes, the subjective *thinking,* or the channel through which the intuitive powers of Uranus flow. This implies the existence of a projective creative level of the mind on the passive receptive level we associate with the subconscious. It is one that is not only a reservoir of creative talent from the past to be tapped, but, one that is impersonal to, and independent of, the feeling nature.

The Moon could be compared to an exoteric activity of the subconscious patterns, rising into our awareness as instinctive emotional reaction and personal memory. Lilith appears to be the esoteric activity of the subconscious, rising into our awareness as instinctive thought response and social memory. Where there is a neurosis, many Lilith researchers have found its seat in the sign and/or house of Lilith. Lilith describes a great deal of what is hidden or indistinct (shadowy) in human nature, or that which seeks gratification above the material consideration or purely emotional gratification.

Through Pluto, the generational challenge marker in the chart, succeeding generations answer to unconscious peer group urges concerning through what (according to sign) to establish further human development along the evolutionary spectrum. Call hearing it the same drummer. It is through Luna, the avenue of the feelings, that they perceive it in an individual way. However, under conditions that call for emotionally mature disciplines, it is Lilith that opens further the subjective feeling nature to the reactive thought nature. In other words, to subconscious thinking along which intuition may naturally flow. It is through Lilith that they know it. This type of mind attunement, or knowing, flows from the subconscious, but from the deeper region of Lilith in the creative desire nature. Lacking a better word, we can call this the subliminal level beyond the immediate emotional level. It's a level that remains darkened (denying) to our total awareness until the mental channels have been cleared of emotional static. Under these conditions, positive talent rises from the social-collective self.

Although Lilith is not easily seen in its daily motion, it is nevertheless perceived by the intuitive eye that translates to the mind the significance of higher activity that is the reality behind unseen forces. There are facets of our character that are not necessarily active in our everyday behavior patterns. As the shadow you cast gives no personal details, in like manner are Lilith characteristics a silhouette of you manifesting impersonally—for instance, through career—as the shadow you cast in the world which is the reality behind you. It is my opinion that we are naive if we expect everything that works on the psychology of the human being to be immediately identifiable in the heavens down to exact detail, anymore than levels of emotional maturity or immaturity are perceived totally with the eye—as Lilith signifies.

As a symbol of the social-collective self, Lilith's demands in our life are for the impersonal approach period. It is for that which occupies the mental, the artistic, the socially productive or the creative approach, or the vocational. This has been demonstrated in hundreds of charts as Lilith's positive level of operation. Where there is emotional immaturity (selfishness) in the character (in the house of Lilith), it represents denial as a discipline. While it is obviously the Moon Luna that commands and supports the personal or subjective motivation, motivation or desire for anything less than impersonal-social desires for Lilith lead to denials pure and simple, i.e., Lilith's level of manifestation is being denied.

The feelings you have of inferiority, or of being victimized, or the unreasoning (blinding) fears of this area in your chart, are indirect results of the lack in emotional maturity needed here for stable perspective. But, are Lilith's denials really a surprise after all? Isn't there the nagging fear of no satisfaction or appreciation here all along? We have found this to be so. What you feel is missing, the apparent void, is Lilith's higher level of values being denied in yourself—by yourself. The static is from something you are not letting go of, and that something is an outgrown dependency or desire where Lilith is located. After all, it is not Lilith, but the Moon Luna that symbolizes subjective desire or response. Lilith symbolizes only the objective thinking approach. Anything less is unsuccessful.

For those who cannot tolerate the hypothetical in planetary discussion, or if one chooses to assume Lilith's total non-existence, it should be remembered that hypothesis is the middle ground between observation and fact.

Specific Orientation
By sign and house position in the natal chart, Lilith has been found to indicate exactly where, through what, or through whom, emotional objectivity or its lack in the individual makeup, is manifested. For the emotionally naive (misdirected), Lilith is indeed the frustration and/or the nagging sense of denial or debilitating experience for which its activity patterns were consistently noted from earliest observations. It is separative, disruptive or flatly denying when motivated from the lower personal levels of selfish desire or selfinterest. However, Lilith is incredibly effective for the intellect, or as a talent stimulus, when operating on the impersonal higher levels of the mind or the creative imagination, particularly when in aspect to Uranus or Saturn. There is dynamic release of intellectual, creative, or esthetic energy when the motivation in the sign holding Lilith is activated in line with realistic and impersonal approaches.

For the emotionally objective, mature person—and note that I did not say controlled, but, rather, objective or detached—Lilith has been found to be a blessing in releasing positive social talent through house position, and a particular area of interest by sign. By sign, the exaggeration of the drive needs the vocational outlet for socially acceptable releases, as discussed in the following section.

Lilith, whose action is quite the opposite of our first Moon, being non-reflective (to our mundane awareness) and more psychological in action, appears from investigation to do with one's social orientation, one's universal concerns, and one's vocation—matters which are as basically objective in nature as the domestic Moon's are subjective. The effect of Lilith's ray is comparable to that of the Moon's only in that they are both instinctive drives; but Lilith is infinitely more commanding in its action. Once released, Lilith tends to be extreme—not unlike Pluto—on either the positive or the negative level. No middleground here. When motivated from self-serving levels of gain (ego or material gratification), Lilith is noted for anything from frustration, upset and shock, to seeming cruel experience or incredibly rebellious behavior. The negative pattern is built up over a period of time by continually denying conditions; hidden resentment of feeling overshadowed or unappreciated; the nagging fear of never having enough; or an undermining inferiority complex.

On the selfish level of desire, Lilith creates unreasoning fears that are understandable when you consider that Lilith rules the intellectual/creative soul aud is entirely disassociated from sentiment or desires of the flesh. It is said that Lilith is like something inhuman? To a certain extent, I suppose we could look at it this way if we consider that humanness in a person or within an emotional situation must necessarily be subjective (Moon). That would be simplistic. It implies a static condition. There must be an area in the chart where emotional growth is promoted as part of the evolving process through understanding or the creative approach. This is the underlying reason for Lilith's particular denials—to promote just that. Since there is nothing subjective about Lilith, unlike the personal orientation and the subjecting desires of the Moon, Lilith *needs* creative motivation or interest in the house it is in for outlets of the mind, spirit, or imagination in contrast to Luna's personal approach through the mundane or the emotional. So we see that when unfulfilled the negative exaggeration is due to the nonuse of the energy which, like any dynamic ray unreleased, builds up in the house it occupies to erupt that way one day.

Through forced circumstances where necessary, Lilith is the emotionally maturing factor that exposes and purges childish expectancies or incredibly naive attitudes in our desire nature through its house matters or the persons) of that house. To quote Bert Bliss (Robert Hurzt Granite), long time researcher of Lilith, "What Lilith is actually doing, is ripping the veil that separates the known world from the unknown world, and letting the individual look out into the reality from whatever level they have been able to attain in their inner world—kind of a 'you asked for it, so see it like it is' kind of an arrangement." He further says, "When the fears of Lilith are faced, her position in the chart becomes the pathway and open door to a higher and more spiritual understanding (that opens the Pandora's Box of your own creativity). The bogey-man in the closet turns out to be the Raggedy Ann doll you forgot you left there." Interpret the 'doll' as the sentimental euphoria you mistook for reality that becomes impossible in the outer circumstances of your life that reject it, and are thus ultimately either intensely subjecting, frustrating, or disillusioning.

Lilith is anathema to subjective attachment. Its equal and opposite rewards come from intellectual awareness and/or creative detachment; in other words, depersonalized orientation in dealing with the matters or persons there. Higher attitudes are constantly being prompted by Lilith into one's awareness through the sinking fears of denial that inhabit and inhibit one who is selfishly oriented here, whether or not he is conscious of it and no matter how socially justifiable it may seem. These desires are stagnating to his continued emotional maturing. They create eye-opening situations one is abruptly faced with or, depending on the chart that one continually faces. These situations eventually force one to grow up and leave behind those comfortable and cherished but totally naive dreams. The doll of the past is just that—a painted smile on an outgrown toy.

To conclude that Lilith's malefic effect is the only valid one, because of the substantial evidence for its negative action, is to deny that there is nothing in nature without a decisive cause or without some relevancy to the whole. Lilith is not the exception to the rule. It has been the outgrown emotional factor that Lilith denies (facilitating the further maturation of the individual) that has eluded interpretation. It has been Lilith as the principal of liberation from the emotional past that has eluded interpretation, explaining a great deal about the emotional conflicts one experiences in the house of Lilith when negative. The negative factor was unfortunately the more obvious one previously. Understandably, the emphasis on the why of it could not be sufficiently concentrated upon in earlier investigations until more was understood of Lilith's total nature. This hopefully puts into proper perspective the conclusions thus far drawn about Lilith's supposed one-sided action. Hopefully, where the rulerships of Lilith *by sign* are concerned, it also explains the unusual talent that may arise through the more naturally impersonal environment of the vocation.

It may sound too qualified for our intellectual comfort, to accept that Lilith's principle is to develop the kind of growing-up or sophistication that can only come from depersonalization through interests that are above purely mundane satisfactions, i.e., for intellectual or creative satisfaction and gain. Nevertheless, I have consistently found its positive effects this way. This has been found to be the "open sesame" for Lilith's incredibly productive level of operation, appearing reasonably automatic for the naturally detached individual—and the underlying reason for problems in others. To a certain extent, we all lack objectivity about ourselves, for one reason or another. Somewhere in our chart is contained our naive expectations and where sentimentally is still entertained. Look to the house that holds Lilith and determine if personal conditions there are problematical. If this is the case, be assured that Lilith is indicating overpersonalization (selfishness) as the underlying reason for the problem that is negatively influencing relationships or matters. Regardless of aspects, until desires shift to higher goals, there is an insistent sense of continued (signaling) denial in the usual satisfactions. The opposite is true when one is successful in depersonalizing here.

When ignorantly mishandled Lilith proves to be as disillusioning to our defensive human frailties as do, for the most part, all of the individualizing rays beyond Saturn. The baser drives we voluntarily or involuntarily cling to become focused. Lilith's frustrated energy turns in on itself to negate the house, creating deadends. At best for the positive individual, but one who nevertheless still remains selfishly motivated in the house of Lilith, continual denials are felt. The light is literally darkened to the self-seeker. The darkness results in the experiencing of our own self-imposed limitations initially begun through the lack of sound emotional judgment. Lilith symbolizes where we are driven to accept or demonstrate responsibility in our actions and reactions in order to mature the desire nature within, as Saturn matures the physical nature without. The goal is to achieve the necessary level, at a given time in the consciousness, for greater growth and positive direction in the emotional life. Lilith's purging experiences act as the concrete form of discipline toward that end.

Like Saturn, Lilith lays no claim to sympathy for human weakness or sentiment. It was Dante Gabriel Rosetti who said:

> "It was Lilith, the first wife of Adam
> Not a drop of her blood was human,
> But she was made like a soft sweet woman."

Lilith creates an allure to whatever is our selfish dream, in order to destroy it for the more creative one you harbor deep in your subconscious. Let us consider the emotional discipline and thus the forced stabilization Lilith introduces, as we similarly consider Saturn in this same function for the material/physical direction that we must face up to, or else experience denial. It was Sepharial who first drew attention to a certain affinity between Lilith and Saturn. Both are obviously disciplining (stabilizing) forces where there is misdirection: Lilith having to do with the desire nature and Saturn having to do with the material nature. As Saturn purges mismanaged material affairs, Lilith purges negative desire. Both are control factors when operating at the lower point. Every human being will eventually attract or be attracted by conditions or persons of like development as himself in the Lilith area—as is the case with any eventually planetary motivator in a house. Through the experiences that result, emotional objectivity is forced or is prompted through frustration, hopefully leaving one the wiser.

We all have varying degrees of environmentally or otherwise programmed subjective responses, where emotional inroads are easily made into our lives and where coping is difficult. This is the classic Lilith when negative. As we become less desirous of selfish gain in the house and sign of Lilith and more desirous of creative, humanitarian, intellectual, or spiritual satisfaction, or for relationships that renew another in one of these directions, it consistently appears that conditions are either automatically bettered or are at the least more wisely judged. This is the key that turns Lilith into the beneficial stimulus that introduces us to the higher worlds of the mind, creativity, or psychic realms. It releases great pools of inspired talent into the consciousness to further creative growth in the individual or someone associated with a particular house.

When one is emotionally liberated from the personal ego enough to view his situation with cold-facts analysis, intellectually or philosophically, then one is automatically satisfying Lilith's compulsion for the sophistication of detachment that must be born into this area of his consciousness. To this extent Lilith's higher level has a strong affinity with Uranus. Both are liberating and strongly individualizing rays. We should not overlook the soul progress that takes some above average readings, and take into consideration the greater universal scope of those who demonstrate the talent releases of this intuitive channel because of having successfully impersonalized their interests here, or raised them to creative scope.

Symbolically, Lilith represents the liberated woman who is responsive to the social unit in contrast to Luna symbolically representing the subjective woman who is responsive to the domestic unit. Lilith liberates, Luna domesticates (the first would rule the E.R.A., the second would rule the P.T.A.). Feminist liberation movements have brought out the clear division of the two general types of women: the objective working professional seeking full socio-economic recognition under the law opposed in principle to the subjective domestic type who fears the loss of her domestic security. Lilith rules social reform (again, channeling the Uranian principle), and equality based on achievement rather than rank in the social structure—the philosophy of the feminist movement in principal.

Facts About Lilith
- Lilith has two clear levels: Clearly positive for creative, mental or esthetic release, and clearly negative, or denying, within the self-centered mundane or emotionally influenced motivation, as Lilith is dark to the subjective eye and enlightening to the objective eye.
- Lilith's energy manifests positively only as a distinctly impersonal force, as opposed to Luna's distinctly personal one.
- Lilith describes the impersonal needs of the social-collective self, whereas Luna describes the emotional needs of the self.
- Lilith is an emotionally maturing force and alien to sentiment.
- Lilith moves you to extremes on either the positive or the negative level.
- Where Lilith is, there is fascination.

- Lilith creates exaggerated susceptibility to the desire nature on subjective levels, emotional repression or unreasonable fears.
- Lilith has affinity with Saturn. Both represent disciplined circumstances that force realistic attitudes: the first emotionally, the second materially. Not unlike Saturn, Lilith demands the not-self approach.
- Lilith's effect limits negative emotionalism as Saturn limits mismanaged material affairs. Both are control factors at the lower level.
- Lilith is the principle of impersonality; whereas it is the Moon Luna that is the principle of personality.
- Lilith depersonalizes.
- Lilith frustrates the self to liberate the social-collective self.
- The house Lilith occupies indicates where one must deal with his own reflections of emotional immaturity when negatively motivated.
- The house Lilith occupies indicates where one must overcome naive or childish expectancies.
- Lilith demands depersonalization in the house it motivates, or with the person(s) of that house to maintain or establish perspective.
- Lilith represents *raw urges* that are for the most part hidden in the personal orientation lest the individual expose a part of himself he does not understand, making him vulnerable or to appear strangely different.
- Creative talent according to sign influences the vocation, distinguishing the person's work from others in the field. In many instances, it may represent the vocation itself.
- Lilith magnifies the energy of whatever planet or point it aspects.
- Lilith is not unlike Uranus. It responds strongly to aspects with this planet, as also to Mars and Saturn.
- Lilith's action in charts parallels Uranus-Pluto actions, but through instinctive *thought* hidden deeply in the depth of the character, to emerge abruptly, unpredictably, compulsively.
- Lilith is exalted in Gemini. It has its fall Sagitarrius. Lilith is dignified in Capricorn. It has its detriment in Cancer.
- Lilith's synodical period is 177 days. It returns to the same longitude on the same day every 126 years according to Sepharial, from observation of the Earth satellites supplied by Dr. Waltemath. Its lesser cycle is 63 year. Its period is 119 days.
- Lilith travels 3°02′ a day in mean motion, approximately 10 days to a sign and roughly four months to travel through the zodiac.
- Where Lilith is placed, there is something shadowy in the personality.
- Lilith has to do with areas of our consciousness that we are not aware of in ourselves.
- In the house of Lilith is where we are forced to outgrow our emotional dependencies.
- When living in the higher nature Lilith specializes talent and greatly sharpens the mind.

- Lilith releases a unique social talent by house position, and a specialty interest by sign that seeks outlet in or through the vocation.
- When negative, it brings susceptibility to strange influences, unusual fascinations, infatuations, or compulsions.
- On subjective levels, Lilith introverts. On objective levels, Lilith extroverts.
- Lilith is the priestess in woman, the individualizing side of woman. It does not have its greater power in the ordinary, but rather in the extraordinary or creative.

Keywords

Basic	*Positive*	*Negative*
Exaggerates	Detachment	Distortion
Magnifies	Independence	Denial
Objectifies	Emotional maturity	Unreasoning fear
Driving	Sophistication	Repression
Challenging	Objectivity	Frustration
Abrupt	Career ambition	Subjecting
Compulsion	Liberating	Emotional immaturity
Overstatement	Depersonalization	Naivete
Extreme	Intellectual or creative expression	Childish expectancies
Impersonal	Lilith's talent level	Purging
Rapid change	Sure guide to spiritual realms	Inhibiting
Raw urges	Specialization	Disrupting
Instinctive reason	Metaphysical talent	Cancelling
Social-collective	Universality	Demoralizing
Independent	Humane	Debilitating
	Genius	Inferiority complex
	Social awareness	Lilith's lower fear level
	Super charm	Alluring
	Persuasive	Hysteria
	Charismatic	Delusion
	Intelligence	Infatuating
	Vision	Illicit
	Intuitive	Feeilng "freaky"
	Gifted	Blinding

Rulerships

Basic	Positive	Negative
Feminist movements	Equal Rights Amendment	White slavery
The Mistress	The Japanese geisha	The Prostitute
Abortions	Medically approved abortion clinics	Back street abortions and child abuse
Lesbians		
Temptation	Career women	The office wife or the other woman
Female equality	Female activists	
Free love philosophy	Community property laws	Feminine betrayal or seduction
Unusual births	Sex education and contraception	
Social reforms	Out-of-wedlock births	The double standard
Co-rules the air in the body and its circulation	Abolition of child labor laws, and rights for women to vote and serve on juries	Illicit sex and rape
		Crib death and blue babies
Wild cats	Oxygen masks and mouth-to-mouth resuscitation	Pornography and adult book stores
The Shrew		Fainting
Bats, particularly the vampire bat	Nudist colonies	Putrid smells of the body
		Hyperventilation
Animals that devour their young		Asphyxiation
		Strangling
Snakes that inhabit trees		Red light districts
		Compulsions
		Strange influences
		Infatuations

Night birds such as the owl and the nighthawk or bullbat, the catbird and nightingale, the sacred ibis of ancient Egypt, the albatross, the crow and the raven, the shrike or butcherbird known for its screeches and shrieks, the black swan of Australia and certain domestic pigeons having an owl-like head, eyes and frill.

For many years preceding the offical discovery of a new planet or satellite, its influence begins to affect mass awareness just as the shadow of things to come precedes an event. It brings forward in the social structure the issues it rules for the necessary changes to begin taking place. The renewed battle for the century old women's bill was not coincidental in the late 1970s to the reported renewal of interest in Lilithian investigations being taken up in Russia since the 1960s.

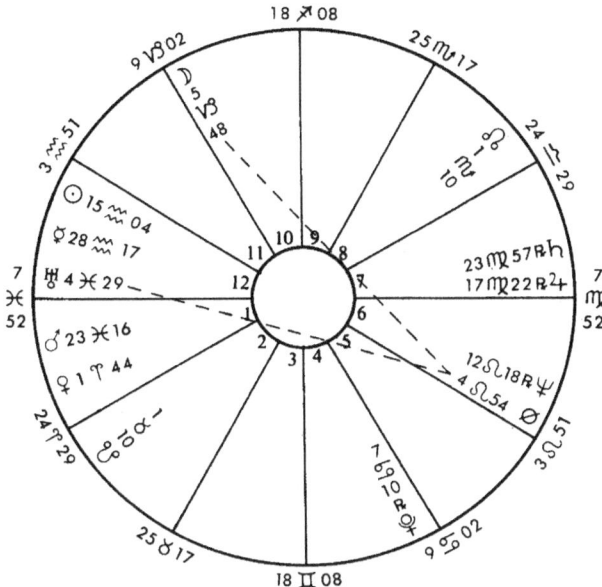

Chart 1. Betty Friedan, Locality Chart, February 4, 1921,

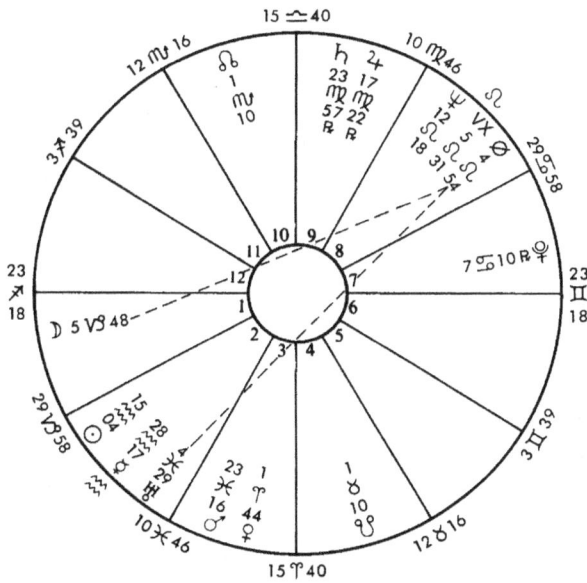

Chart 2. Betty Friedan, Feminist, February 4, 1921, 0400 CST, Peoria, Illinois; Source: Penfield, Rodden

Charts of women in the forefront of the fight for equal rights were found to have a significant position of Lilith. Betty Friedan was a president of the National Organization for Women (NOW). Friedan's Lilith is in Leo, magnifying leadership drive and fixed urges for recognition completely as an individual based on creative or intellectual merit and not on sex (see charts 1 and 2). It is the action point of a yod configuration, with Uranus and the Moon making up the sextile at the other point. The Capricorn Moon, denoting the professional woman, in sextile to Uranus, aptly describes the women's liberation work she so compulsively led. Lilith is conjunct Neptune, significantly describing the title of her book, *The Feminine Mystique*. Lilith in the sixth house in both her solar and Johndro locality charts and square the lunar nodes indicates the acutely personal unrest she felt for the working woman against the traditional ideas of women being subjective to males in intelligence, achievement and compensation. Uranus in Pisces in eighth sign quincunx to Lilith sharply magnified crusading liberationist urges for the minorities. In her natal chart, the Lilithian action point is manifested through the eighth house, marking the regeneration of the old suffragette movement she accomplished.

Friedan was followed by Gloria Steinem, feminine activist and equally dynamic leader of the women's liberation movement. Lilith is on the cusp of Libra/Scorpio opposition Uranus and square Pluto from the twelfth house of confinement and socially handicapped minorities, in this case magnifying the socio-financial inequality of a particular group (see chart 3). Ms. Steinem's fight was for continued pressure to legalize the reform that had been introduced to equalize the feminine position alongside men. Magnified through opposition by Lilith, Uranus (progressive urges) from the sixth house of working conditions opposes Jupiter (legal principles) and squares Pluto (reform)—to bring in by association Lilith's influence to this significant T-square in her chart. The Pluto in Cancer outlet of this T-square in the ninth house of legal principles describes the power struggles she could manipulate on behalf of maneuvering into obsolescence the traditional ideas of women's subserviant role in business and the economy. She helped batter down not only negative attitudes about liberated women, but about negative or guilty attitudes within women themselves through her publication. She was the editor of *Ms. Magazine* that allowed a format in which women were given publicity and could take pride in their achievements. She was a vociferous spokesman for women's legal and social rights. Her dedication to equal rights was a Lilith in Libra outcry positively applied.

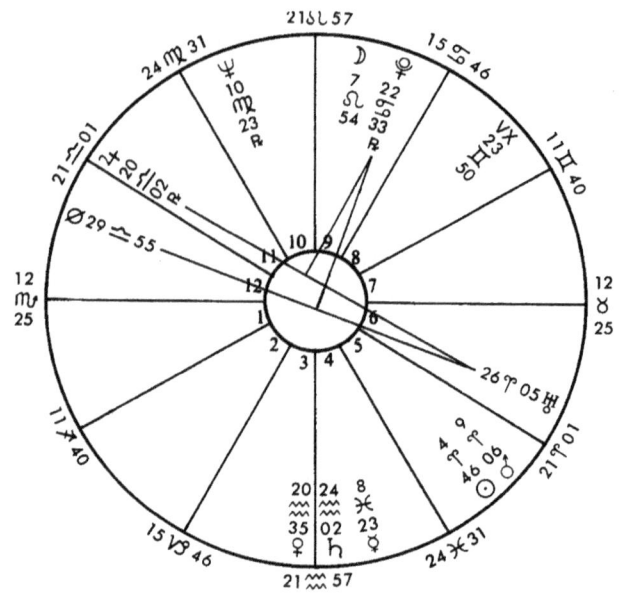

Chart 3. Gloria Steinem, Feminist, March 25, 1934, 2200 EST, Toledo, Ohio; Source: Penfield, Rodden

Black femininist activist Angela Davis has Lilith in Sagittarious conjunct a Venus that is square Neptune from the eighth house, which describes her idealistic and deeply Socialistic attitudes. Opposing Saturn, ruler of the tenth and eleventh houses and trine the Moon in the tenth, Lilith magnified into action her sense of public responsibility toward what she believed could make for a better society, subsequently joining the Communist Party and losing her prestigious teaching position in the psychology department of a California university. On the intellectual level of this opposition, she accomplished a Ph.D in psychology. On the personal level, with Lilith conjunct the chart ruler, Venus, in the eighth house, she was considered a radical and dangerous within the teaching curriculum of the school (see chart 4).

The Lilith Influence/21

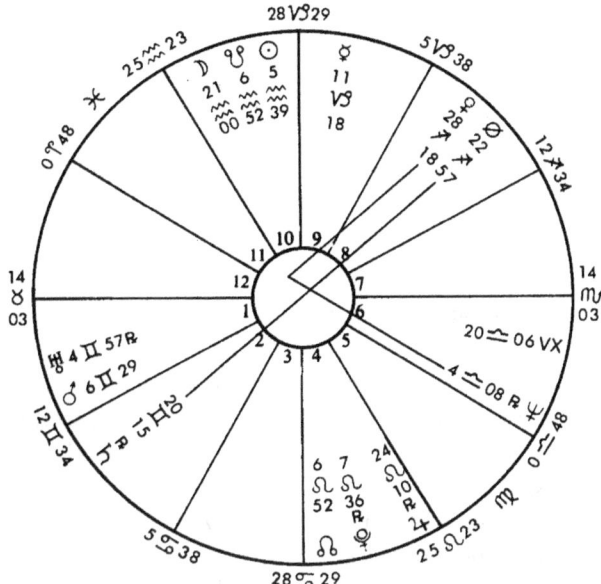

Chart 4. Angela Davis, Militant, January 26, 1944, 12:30 p.m, Birmingham, Alabama; source: B.C. Per Penfield, Jansky

The presently accepted symbol for Lilith is a circle with a diagonal line cutting through the center. This is most significant as it coincides remarkably with conclusions drawn from our observations. The symbolic diagonal line, occultly representing the upright creative man, appears not to allow for much (if any) of the horizontal line involvement that occultly denotes the animal overtones in the cross matter of matter that are basic in man's nature. Also the symbol is said to represent a lesser moon diagonally divided as the cycle of Lilith is divided into half-yearly appearances, with the major cycle being 126 years and the minor cycle 63 years.

Aspects to Lilith can be misleading if one does not take into consideration the levels at which Lilith is operable. When living in the lower nature at the Lilith point, no amount of supportive traits (aspects) seem to assist, although it indicates the ability to become more quickly aware from the experiences as to where or, more importantly, why, he has been deluding himself. Extroverted attitudes for the house matters of Lilith are constantly being challenged forward. When this finally comes about, even the pressures of the square family of aspects are thrust into powerful career or creative channels. The ultra-compelling force becomes dynamically supportive to socio-public goals. This is the illusive quality the shadowy Lilith brings into the chart. Just as the veil of Neptune exaggerates self-serving negativity to disarming depths of disillusionment and positive goals to successful heights, so too are these extremes evident for Lilith.

For affectional relationship activity, the Moon symbolizes emotional patterns made conscious through Venus (attachment)—thus it is exalted in Taurus. However, it is Lilith that symbolizes subliminal "thought" patterns made conscious through Mercury for intellectually suited relationships (detachment)—thus, it is said to be exaltated in Gemini. The fall is given to Sagittarius because the instinctive mental insights must be consciously clarified by the concrete mind of the individual and not left to generalities or further abstractions. Lilith exaggerates; in Sagittarius, exaggeration is compounded. Though the desire for knowledge and truth is intense in these individuals, it can be prematurely disseminated before it is properly seasoned.

Positive effects of Lilith have become more obvious as we rapidly move into the sophisticated technology of the Aquarian Age's more liberated lifestyles, where attitudes are becoming more objective due to the impersonality in which a computerized society is finding itself.

Vocational Orientation
We note the observation that Lilith tends to exaggerate its sign's values, rulerships, and characterstics in the person's makeup. This overstatement appears to lie as deeply within the character as Lilith itself lies shadowy within the scope of the Earth's orbit. The exaggerations are instinctively masked in the nature on the mundane level, lest they be misunderstood or bring rejection. They are revealed through the vocation, somehow, some way—as if in blessed relief. So raw, by comparison to one's outer environment, are these feelings that they are to be kept in the shadows of the personality until a socially acceptable area of release is found for such bold drives. When released through the vocation, or an area of it, they indicate a special talent. When released through an avocation, they indicate a specialized creative expression. Lilith's sign magnification in the makeup is not as a rule detectable in our daily attitudes. In fact, it may very well be made to appear as quite the opposite: undercompensation known by only a few who are close.

During the impressionable and formative early years, we become aware of this difference in our makeup, as compared to others. A child naturally seeks acceptance and later, for the same reason, desires a certain amount of conformity. Therefore, he builds for himself, or is disciplined by others, into automatic stops that become almost an unconscious part of him. This becomes so repressed that it surfaces as a vague sense of something missing all the time in the area of Lilith, or uneasy feelings of denial. Compensatory behavior is automatically demonstrated to direct attention away from the overemphasis that is instinctively feared as being too untempered at the personal level for the conformity which we all seek to one degree or another. Through such repressed feelings where Lilith is located, roots are given to an inferiority complex, until rewards are found through mental pursuits, emotional objectivity, and/or are freed through an area of the vocation, where the impersonal atmosphere transforms it into a special talent within his or her work.

It is in this observation of Lilith's overstatement of its sign's characteristics that I have observed its importance for releases in vocational guidance. Through the lifework, the individual can enjoy a social outlet of a personal dimension that is mundanely suppressed. Lilith's sign characteristics give the difference, or the uniqueness to the career, that sets it apart from another's. Lilith is specialized energy that calls attention to a particular area or special interest within the framework of the vocation.

If the behavior patterns connected to Lilith's sign characteristics are outwardly evident and far out of proportion in the mundane areas of life, the overpull (though he may deny it), or the nagging introverted emphasis of these qualities, obviously suggest not enough opportunity for satisfaction at the daily level. Then, a creative hobby or intellectual pursuit becomes very important. An example would be something like the impersonal Lilith point being in Leo. In order to keep asserting the self as an individual to others, the autocratic or dictating tendencies can be maddening on the personal level, but find gratifying release through something like an evening study group, artistic efforts, or taking a leadership role on behalf of young people or students. The Leo force would not be bottled up and become negative. Quite the contrary, Lilith's equal and opposite magnification would produce more than the positive talent to do it with.

Lilith is exaggeration. Lilith is driving. Lilith promotes the impersonal by denying the personal. Lilith forces detachment by frustrating attachment. Lilith imposes emotional maturity (adult attitudes) by opposing emotional naivete (childish expectancies), wherever its house matters or dealing with the persons of that house is concerned.

Ivy Jacobson stated: "Lilith rules temptations and betrayals that dishonor if sufficiently negative. Then: is susceptibility to strange influences, delusions, fascinations, infatuations and compulsions. Under extreme conditions there are demoralizing and illicit effects, though such a person is not entirely responsible because of the compulsion that finally takes him off guard." Yes, Lilith creates exaggerated vulnerability to the desire nature on subjective levels. Impersonality is naturally blocked within the emotional or materialistic orientation, which is why Lilith is flatly denying of gratification here that builds up to the compulsive behavior. Naivete can be incredible. But, equally and oppositely, Lilith also magnifies the objectivity of the intellectual or esthetic nature when there is sufficient detachment from the personal ego. Lilith's opposite magnification must indeed be the genius potential that is possible through so Uranian-like an expression at its positive pole, particularly when this planet is involved. Lilith is extreme one way or the other.

Self-centered attitudes that underlie the house matters of Lilith attract frustration but of course always in proportion to the extent of one's selfish preoccupation—and usually quite abruptly. Lilith exaggerates, and the abusive effects will have a purging action; but Lilith's progressive effects have a generating action in the other direction. Lilith is talent released at its higher point.

The intuitive and artistic potentials of Lilith had not been fully reported, but they can be followed to show Lilith's strong creative potential successfully objectified through the social collective self or vocation, as discussed in the following sections. By sign they are outwardly defined in the career area, and particularly when stimulated by direction, transit, and/or by eclipse. Once they are prompted forward, they seek to spend themselves compulsively until a certain amount of release is satisfied.

Basically, Lilith is objectification. Its overstatement by sign remains negative in the nature only in proportion to the lack of emotional maturity in the social orientation. Like the stabilizing, though necessarily limiting denials of Saturn upon the physical, we are met with equally like-oriented force at the Lilith point for direction, direction, direction. Both symbols share this affinity within the maturing process; both motivate strong ambition at the higher point.

Treat Lilith as a satellite, or if you must, as a hypothetical planet as did Alan Leo, until its existence is more concretely accepted. However, we should not make the mistake of discounting Lilith's influence totally in the natal chart until we have investigated it thoroughly for ourselves.

In his 1935 astronomical ephemeris, Raphael speaks of the matter being open to his mind because of the constant and frequent practical results and evidence that have been such as to provide the "missing links" that compelled his belief.

Chapter 3

Lilith Through the Signs

Lilith in Aries
Lilith in Aries is found among those who tend to be the frontrunners in their work, or those who are compelled to innovate new frontiers. Self-assertive and forceful in their work, it usually bears the strong stamp of their personality. Staggering energy and competitive power are usually the hallmarks of the career. They are great believers in talent upon demand. Decisiveness and seemingly unlimited resourcefulness, give the executive qualities and powers of offense by which they drive themselves as well as others.

Career initiative appears limitless. Such people may appear as if driven by some inner force. There is a great sense of selfprojection. What might be hyperactivity blessedly released through vocational channels becomes hypertension under stress.

Mohandas Gandhi of India demonstrated that courage can become a supreme factor in the proving grounds of the career. Violence may play a role in the lifework if Lilith is seriously stressed, as in the martyring of John F. Kennedy (see chart 5). Lilith in Aries in a sinister position behind the seventh cusp opposed the Ascendant and squared the Midheaven, and by its association to the Midheaven, Saturn. JFK expressed an exaggerated, if not distorted, courage for his convictions when he refused to stay away from trouble spots known to be dangerous, or to take reasonable precautions. He stated that if an assassin were determined to kill him it, could be done anywhere, whereupon he proceeded to describe how it could be done quite accurately—and was, in Dallas. Lilith sextiled Uranus and squared his lunar nodes. His book, *Profiles in Courage* and his famous rescue swim from a PT109 during the second world war certainly drew attention to his preoccupation with daring and his own personally Lilithian daring behavior.

Both Alan Leo and Evangeline Adams pioneered their field and faced legal battles, rising to new heights as a result. Powerful career thrust and enterprise are distinct characteristics of Lilith exaggerated in inexhaustible Aries. The profession is usually found

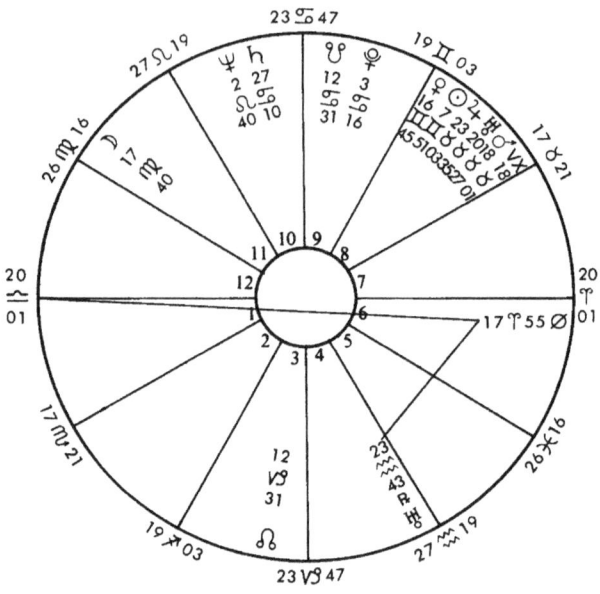

Chart 5. John F. Kennedy, May 29, 1917, 3:00 p.m. EST, Brookline, Massachusetts; source: Marcia Moore

to have some element of risk, pioneering, or leadership in it, such as opening dynamic new areas of thought if it be a literary pursuit, editorializing, or promoting new talent. It may involve troubleshooting for contemporaries, as they are ideal spokesmen in controversy, opening new areas of their chosen field, or leading the fight for personal rights. These are the pathfinders.

Lilith in Aries indicates the overstatement of self for which attempts are made to compensate by an outer charm, and even humility, if necessary. This draws attention away from what the person instinctively prefers to modify in his nature, and keep private this powerful identity complex in those areas where conformity is necessary, even desired. On close inspection one can hardly mistake the personal signature on everything done. Originality receives reverence. A venue through which initiatory urges may be relieved is sought, even promoted.

This is not to imply egotism but, simply an overstated importance put upon self, wherein naturally all things must begin for self and others. Until these people gain enough perspective and perceptive ability to equate their self-esteem with the quality of their knowledge or creative strengths, the denial to admit this personality doubleplus in the mundane areas of life may cause an identity crisis. It is birthed from early feelings of initiative frustration and fear of denial in personal recognition, bringing anything from intense depression to hypertensive states.

Personal rights are considered inalienable, bringing sharp automatic responses under any challenge. However, be assured that when positively released, i.e., when there is objectivity about themselves for good social orientation, this right is also given to others and tremendous respect for initiative is given accordingly. If the chart is benevolent enough otherwise, the way is actually paved by one with Lilith in Aries for the release of this same initiative in others. Incidentally, though it accounts for exuberant enthusiasm that gives the appearance of a coquette or flirtatiousness at times, this is not necessarily the case.

Impulsiveness and temper on the mundane levels are explained away under the guise of some exigency—and this is probably so, but oh what a blessed relief. The not ordinarily obvious "do it my way" syndrome is definitely there and strong, as those who accidentally run up against it can verify. In Aries, Lilith makes the personality so vigorous, that the usual personality markers of the Ascendant and the Moon appear to stamp the nature more severely than the Sun position.

Fear of denial of personal identity or initiative-release during the impressionable and plastic early years is at the bottom of the identity complex that results in exaggeration later on. Once release is gratifyingly found for this strong identity preoccupation, through relating the self through extroverted channels as in teaching, writing or the arts, the power of Lilith is no longer denied. It then compulsively generates the personality thrust into a driving creative force to be reckoned with in the chosen field. The ability to raise their sights above personal concerns to social concerns, and to view the self as objectively as one might view another, will untangle many frustrations in relationships and denials of personal gratifications.

People with Lilith in Aries

Evangeline Adams	Howard Hughes	Irving Berlin	Aldous Huxley
Walter Brennan	John F. Kennedy	Paul G. Clancy	Robert Kennedy
Salvador Dali	Alan Leo	Bette Davis	Marconi
Albert Einstein	Pablo Picasso	Clark Gable	Lowell Thomas
Mohandas Gandhi	Noel Jan Tyl		

Lilith in Taurus

Lilith in Taurus overstates the security consciousness and the personal standards. It registers an intense need for beauty with quality and timelessness in the deepest awareness of the individual. It underscores a deep admiration and profound respect for prosperity, value, and harmony in whatever form. Personal values on whatever level, be they material, moral, intellectual, or esthetic, are of such magnitude as to be kept in the shadows of this one's nature, lest a truly raw need within the self be exposed and then denied. The root of this exaggerated sense of personal worth, and intense desire to enjoy the beautiful and the durable in life, lies so deep in the consciousness as to foster repressed fears of denial. The cheap or tawdry is personally offensive to the sensitive need for excellence in form or sound, which belies a seemingly outward lack of emphasis, but doesn't escape the notice of those in close relationships.

No matter the amount of wealth or goods one may amass, these people will never feel satisfied if they are not relating their personal sense of worth to values above the material, or to intellectually gratifying areas such as the impersonal world of the literary to free the mind, or the arts to free the soul. To do otherwise denies Lilith's compelling higher value urges in Taurus and is as frustrating as attempting to satisfy a tree with a single cup of water. Lilith has no satisfying release on superficial levels, just as it is a shadow against the Sun to our superficial eye. But it is perceived through the eye of the imagination (creative mind) or the spirit (esthetic need).

The ordinary survival or prestige standards of gain are but a mere shadow of where this person's higher sense of security in himself must come from. In order to become a socially mature individual, these people's needs are to seek wealth in life through talents as well as virtues that seed harmony and beauty around themselves and others, and through recognizing that the products of the mind and imagination are as precious and as real as uncut gems are to anyone else. This is necessary in order to free themselves of nagging insecurity fears that are felt from what are obviously values now that are too shallow for their further emotional growth.

In the mechanical areas of living, the compelling urge "to have" is hidden under a veil of conformity as a defense from childhood, due to the apparent disproportion from others. One senses this (or it is brought to his or her attention) during the impressionable years of the automatic comparisons children make to one another. This sensitive, raw part of their makeup is repressed for reasons ranging from the youthful fear of being different from their peers, to fears of denial from their elders who might not understand. It inhibits feelings of being loved or of making personal choices through which he is able to judge the worth of themselves in the world later on. If a suitable outlet for blessed release here is found through some area of the vocation, or as the vocation itself, then determination, discrimination, follow-through and endurance become characteristics in the makeup toward both success in career and the ability to feel love.

Earning ability through artistic, mental, or creative output; developing appreciation for the esthetic in quality, or preserving the beautiful in whatever form are all tied to the personal sense of security. An insecurity complex persistently nags from within if the search for self-worth is only tied to the material and the emotional ego appetites. In the former, we have three prominent writers and a journalist listed in the examples following.

There is a compelling urge for beauty as the purest form of truth. For those inclined to the literary life, it is the perfection of Being that they seek to portray or teach with words. Through the artistic, in whatever form it takes, whether it be through the pursuit of theatre, music, crafts, or as a valid supporter of the arts, there is deep satisfaction because the Taurean longing for lasting quality, tone, or beauty is being compensated for. In turn, it builds a lasting sense of soul worth that is the ultimate possession, as opposed to transitory material wealth. Music as the aristocracy of sound, or literature as the aristocracy of thought, give one with Lilith in Taurus the feeling of ultimate security he feared he would never know. In Taurus, Lilith works through denial of superficial satisfactions of gain, for the impersonal but more lasting literary or esthetic values that finally bring to this one emotional objectivity, inspiration and that delicious sense of freedom that only satisfied security desires can bring.

The basic drive of a Taurean Lilith, and to a great extent for its house position in the second, is to promote a socially mature attitude for the *why* of the material goods of the world instead of for the *what,* showing it as a means to an end and not as an end in itself. Objectivity in personal values is forced through constant feelings of "being poor," to quote Phyllis Dee Harrison, and nagging secret anxieties of having missed something—be he truck driver or king.

This is one of the finest positions in the chart for materializing truth and beauty in the form world. The stamp of quality is the signature of one with Lilith in Taurus.

People with Lilith in Taurus

C.E.O. Carter	Maurice Chevalier	Henry Ford	Llewellyn George
Helen Hayes	Charles Lindbergh	Eleanore Roosevelt	Dane Rudhyar

Lilith in Gemini

Lilith in Gemini is a particularly excellent sign placement. The mental magnification urges the mind to so lucid a level, as to move it along in the world of thought, oblivious to surroundings, while probing the delights of imaginative focusings. Mental reverie is indulged in, for the mind to roam freely back and forth over experiences or conversations in order to savor them; to focus on them more clearly, or to simply relax in the imagination to see what ideas may eventually surface to be deliciously pondered. The imaginative powers of the mind are strong and logical, making way for creative thought or novel literary talent.

There is the capacity to stay slightly above the reach of the emotional in relationships, so that the mental freedom to move in any direction is never totally hindered. It is rare that these people are seriously influenced by others, because they simply accept as their inalienable right to think as they wish, respecting this in others as well. They are open to valid suggestion, which is independently scrutinized by the mind's eye at leisure. They are capable of a rare sense of humor. The comical in life may be ingeniously emphasized, as in the case of the successful comedian Red Skelton. The genius factor of this position may be focused into brilliance, as in the case of Werner Von Braun, considered the foremost rocket engineer of his times.

We note the physical manifestations of Lilith in Gemini: something unusual about the hands or fingers. There may be great strength, unusual sensitivity or healing in the hands; they may be heavily veined, the fingers in some instances double-jointed, or possessing psychometrizing talent—particularly if Lilith is also in the third and water signatures are strong.

In Gemini, Lilith is one of the finest positions for prompting objectivity, as both the sign and the planet represent reasoning processes. The former for the concrete mind and the latter for the instinctive subconscious that channels psychological (instinctive mental) activity forward.

The exaltation for the mental probes of Lilith in Gemini, or its accidental exaltation in the third house, is logical. The fall in Sagittarius is applicable, since the Lilithian impulses, being exaggerated enough already, need to be factually and concretely clarified, as opposed to the ninth sign abstractions, where the overstatement of Lilith seriously risks the abandon of detailed investigation. Lilith is subliminal, or apart enough from concrete existence to be not as efficiently channeled in philosophical Sagittarius, where data is not easily applied, where the insights could be left to such abstractions as religion, where they may become lost in dogma; or philosophy, where they become lost in theory. Aspects from Saturn assist in anchoring conceptual direction for Lilith in Sagittarius.

While appearing to be an attentive listener, people with a Gemini Lilith can mentally move almost totally into another area for more mental food to absorb. Disinterest is tactfully masked to avoid appearing impolite, which is not the intention at all. The focusing tendencies given to the mind simply search for more gratifying subjects that will satisfy urgings for the diverse and the novel. This becomes so much a habit that it is done quite unconsciously, although, it isn't entirely unnoticed by close associates.

Early in life, people with Lilith in Gemini may credit others with their unique ideas, as they feel no qualification by which they can explain having them. It appears that by doing this they avoid the exposure of something about their mind they have not yet learned to handle in themselves. Strange, but true. Not so however, in later years, where they seek outlet, usually through the vocation, to satisfy the mental probes. At the very least, Lilith in Gemini surfaces through an unusual, above-normal manual dexterity. Their talented hands are for a specific purpose, such as those with outstanding ability as surgeons or builders of highly sensitive technical equipment, musicians, massage therapists, and diagnosticians. They have educated fingers.

People with Lilith in Gemini are capable of brilliant recitations, as in the case of actor Charles Laughton. They are readers and are the ones most apt to take a book along wherever they go if they anticipate the need to fill mental voids. Those with Lilith in Gemini never appear bored. They may mentally climb the Himalayas or contemplate a past experience in greater detail. The attention span is impressive if the subject matter holds fascination. There are strong powers of the logical in the imagination, to take the individual out beyond the obvious to the inobvious. A sense of the ridiculous or the comedy of life is ever with them. They recognize what "Puck" said on the cover of the Sunday Comic Sections years ago, "What fools we mortal be." The emotional objectivity or detachment this person is capable of reaching, eventually frees him from the programmed conditioning of ideas we are automatically impressed with as children. They can explore the novel freely through the powerful focus from which they can direct the imagination's probings in order to bring back the unusual or the diverse in ideas or composition.

People with Lillith in Gemini

Lucille Ball	Carrie Jacobs Bond	Werner Von Braun	Reinhold Ebertin
Jackie Gleason	Rube Goldberg	Max Heindel	Charles Laughton
Grant Lewi	Albert Schweitzer	Red Skelton	Sydney Omarr

Lilith in Cancer

Lilith in Cancer magnifies the natural emotional responsiveness and mediumistic tendencies of Cancer, and exaggerates accordingly the defensiveness in the makeup against emotional intrusion or confrontation. Emotional fortification is usually well established by adulthood, although hidden in the personality. A firm but gracious fluctuating mobility of consideration emerges, enabling this person to fluidly shift attention away from any area coming up that he cannot handle. This is done so affably and usually becomes so much of an unconscious effort (defense mechanism) that it appears entirely natural, to all that is, but a perceptive few close to the individual.

The tactical defenses of people with Lilith in Cancer are, of course, colored by the basic temperament of the chart itself. For example, if Scorpio is predominant, when all else fails the defense may be to simply remove themselves from the situation as swiftly as possible, or never to have appeared in the first place if such is anticipated. There is the defense of the more diplomatic departure or tactical fence mending at any price of Libra; the doubletalk or errand to be run of Gemini; or the open hostility of Aries if the sensitive antenna of Lilith in Cancer is picking up bad weather ahead. This is not intended to be dishonest, but rather it is to protect the self from possible inroads that people are not yet emotionally objective enough to deal with.

Long ago they sensed their phenomenal crab-like soft center and have built in a compensating personality plus of gracious congeniality and hospitality in order to insure calm waters in their environment. There is a defensive hostility in their depths that protects the magnified sensitivity, which is usually unknown to others because of polite maneuverings to transform matters to more comfortable emotional limits. Importance is put on etiquette and approved social manners, i.e., Emily Post, an authority on the subject who influenced social behavior with her book *Etiquette: The Blue Book of Social Usage*.

What may appear as only an inconvenience to another, overstates itself as an upset to those with Lilith in Cancer. They learn early in life to smoothly move away from even the most minor confrontation. Consideration and congeniality become sincere efforts to create as hospitable an atmosphere as possible. They will bend every effort firmly toward insuring a comfortable atmosphere, because in making you relaxed, *they* can be comfortable with *you*. The home is very important. They appear unable to function unless it is organized or run to their satisfaction. It is a prime necessity to their inner peace, and is by no means a small consideration in their lives.

The impression is given of moving through life with as little disruption as possible. It is the better part of valor to cooperate with the settings those with Lilith in Cancer create, or soon one will run up against their guard. Unlike Lilith in Aries, which is tactically aggressive, Lilith in Cancer is tactically defensive. This does not lessen the sincerity and kindness, but is simply their way of insuring smooth waters for all concerned, and primarily for themselves.

You see, in Cancer, Lilith magnifies subjectivity until, or unless, the powers of analysis are developed enough to supply the objectivity they need to feel less vulnerable. There can be phenomenal naivete (childish expectancies), while assuming an outward worldliness that belies the truth. Confident detached behavior, to demonstrate poise, eventually has them even believing themselves, until a time when the vulnerability under the surface is cracked from some situation strong enough to break their denial of this sensitivity. They then can feel as exposed as if they were suddenly stripped naked. In turn, this forces them, defensively, to understand the situation in order to live with it, analyze it, or somehow to come to terms with it, in order to adjust themselves against any such future happenings.

Lilith's disarming effects take many forms, but they basically result in proportion to Lilith's non-release through a mental, creative or vocational field that takes in Cancer rulership, where interest is most operable and compelling. In such detached areas, these people possess highly marketable talents, and are greatly released from their defensiveness. Putting service above self, analyzing or looking for practical solutions for the person, event or circumstances of the house holding Lilith, frees this one from subjectivity to objectivity, and thus brings gratification. Liken this position to a Scorpio Moon, with the difference being that the vulnerability of Lilith in Cancer is a psychological thing, whereas with the Scorpio Moon it is a conscious thing. In both, the extreme need is to depersonalize.

There is an uncanny talent for spotting trends, executive mobility, a tenacity that creates dependability and follow-through, wisdom in strengthening foundations or establishing them well; occult or medical (nursing) orientation, working in child care areas; and the ability to fluctuate smoothly with public demands. Anyone of these may play a significant role in the vocation. It is in the areas where outlets for these and other Cancer talents can be found that the individual feels more fulfilled, released, and happier.

If this person is in legal work, courtroom defense as opposed to prosecution would be preferred; if an artist, there is unique talent for ocean scenes or water colors; if in music, he or she can portray emotional pathos in sound; if in the military, he or she does better in something like the defense-oriented Coast Guard rather than the offense-oriented Marines; if he or she is literary, the writings are of a foundational nature for the security of the chosen subject, as we find in the great work of Marc Edmund Jones; or publicly oriented, as we have in the contributions of Dal Lee.

People with Lilith in Cancer

Ethel Barrymore	William Beebe	Dal Lee	Madame Curie
Queen Elizabeth II	Barry Goldwater	Marc Edmund Jones	Bert Lahr
Stephen Vincent Benet	Alfred Nobel	J.C. Penney	Emily Post

Lilith in Leo

Lilith in Leo exaggerates a sense of individualism in the makeup that results in the tendency to pick up the reins of leadership or management in whatever field is chosen. Creatively expressive and willfully assertive, they attract followers or projects they need, and find great pleasure in guiding or in the management of them, at whatever level they are operating. When self-interest dominates the character, dictating tendencies that continually focus their will upon others can be maddening on the personal level, and eventually create the very denial of individual expression he or she is so deeply desires.

The deep instinct (as a nagging fear) to avoid being just another face in the crowd, and risk denial of total freedom in the individual expression of his or her will, forces an exaggerated sense of centerstage. It surfaces as autocratic tendencies if the one with Lilith in Leo even suspects himself or herself of being overshadowed by the environment, as those close to them can testify. Areas that can be needful and fulfilling are the educational world, various areas of the entertainment field with its myriad creative crafts for the mind or imagination; or for a management or governing position in which leadership can be intellectually, creatively or at least outwardly channeled. These people could spiral an avocation or special hobby into an important part of their work, or eventually as the vocation itself, because of the compelling drive behind the creative ego when Lilith is in the fifth sign.

Acute individualism or a feeling of specialness—standing out from the crowd—is so primary a part of these people's nature as to have them veil its existence from others in the early years for fear of being too noticeably non-conforming, that they risk rejection or misunderstanding. This inner self-denial begins in the dependencies of childhood, where the immediate need is for acceptance from others, which is largely gained through learned conformity. The magnified will, deep in its makeup, is outwardly repressed from others, even successfully from themselves for a time, until these individuals can deal with the aristocratic feelings that make them feel so different from others. In the character traits of the sign that Lilith exaggerates, these individuals are unusual, and rather than risk denial, these people drive the trait within through behavior that masks this in their nature, or by attempts to block the trait in their nature for a time. Such blocking (sometimes consciously and sometimes not), as children are capable of doing in order to protect their delicate psyche, is common enough in special instances depending on the chart, but it appears to be the usual manner in which people veil over these raw Lilithian (by sign) urges lest they draw opposition or problems for something in themselves they cannot yet handle or understand.

What might be leadership super-urges relieved through career position, or creative expression released through a profession, when under stress due to lack of outlet, can become backache or heart trauma. By reflex action in the fixed cross, they may become leg pains, throat problems or problems in the regenerative organs. This is particularly so if Lilith is in the sixth or first house, or in close aspect with the rulers of these houses. This is not to imply an autocratic nature, but simply an unusually magnified sense of the individual drama about the self that aches for an accepted outlet. However, sincere respect and recognition are given by them for these qualities in others, and in many instances is enthusiastically supported. They are often misunderstood to be egotists. Individualism and self-expressive rights are considered sacred.

Be not mistaken that these people will tolerate denial of repressed traits for long. Thus we have the angry willful release of rebellion as dictatoriallike tendencies when thwarted. The overdramatization or "roaring" about not being appreciated is explained away under the guise of some immediate problem or petty demal that brought it to a head—but oh the joy of letting go to clear the inner air.

Regal or autocratic tones can be heard in the voice when Lilith in Leo aspects Mercury in the chart. When conjunct Venus, or in close aspect, the individuality is never totally surrendered in relationships. This is not good or bad but simply that the individuality is kept inviolable. Mars in close aspect to Lilith gives the kind of leadership dynamics that express themselves for instance through trouble-shooting, no matter the length of time it takes, as in the case of former U.S. Secretary of State Henry Kissinger.

Lilith in Leo people automatically attract followers or disciples when releasing the inner will to outer service. When the strong will is given toward public or socially serving interests, as opposed to self-serving ones, or through vocational outlet that expresses the mind, the artistic or intellectual force, Lilith in Leo becomes a driving ambition in the arts; the entertainment or literary field; education in whatever form it takes; public service or government. Given toward personal power of simply ego satisfactions, they eventually feel Lilith's bitter denials through children, friendship, and love relationships or recognition.

People with Lilith in Leo

Lon Chaney	Cecil B. DeMille	Henry Kissinger	Benito Mussolini
William Hearst	Ann Blyth	Eugene Ormandy	Grace Metalious

Lilith in Virgo

With Lilith in Virgo there is exaggerated anxiety concerning detail, due to the magnification of the abstract qualities of the mind. The intensity to apply technique is obvious in the sometimes irrational irritability those close to these people encounter when they are concentrating. Acute sensitivity to detail can cause these people to feel beaten before they begin a project. The exaggerated conscientiousness that Lilith creates in Virgo gives rise to unreasonable fears, thus emotional anxiety about the ability to handle it. This may be screened by much time given to elaborate preparations that are all out of proportion to the task. Therapeutic relaxation is found in hobbies that call for intricate application of small parts or pieces. Amplified concern about the minute details involved in matters that are feared may be beyond them, underlies a carefully hidden defeatist attitude. This may be outwardly compensated for by an air of complacency or proclaimed disinterest. This is, at the very least, noticeable early in life, lest these people expose their own self-judged weakness. They find apparent security in rationalization whenever they fear being inadequate to the precision or details involved. Reverence for a job or work perfectly done by others stamps their own exaggerated desire of such expression.

Though they may inwardly feel overwhelmed by the myriad details necessary to run daily life smoothly to their satisfaction, if an abstract skill such as trigonometry were necessary for a career in healthcare, creative, or social work, they are apt to breeze right through it. This is not at all the contradiction it sounds like, because it is the vocational factor of detachment that makes the difference. The exaggerated perfectionism is more apt to be negative in the subjective personal areas of life, because of the emotional considerations that distract and, in this case, negate their concentration. There is great nervous tension lest any detail be missed, sometimes making their resulting inefficiency take on near comical proportions. Lilith demands detachment (the impersonal approach) or it will frustrate any order the individual attempts to bring about. Lilith gives more positive results when expressing detail through the vocation, because of the detachment possible under these circumstances, when only the job at hand is to be considered in which case the precision drive is remarkably well released.

To alleviate emotional tension or simply to relax these people may often find themselves carefully counting things—any thing—just to satisfy the need for orientation to detail that has an emotionally calming effect. Otherwise, they are known to overstate detail upon detail for repetition, repetition, repetition during the times when they are either in fear of being distracted, or the conversation upsets their concentration. It then tends to become a one-sided conversation—a monologue—allowing for no interruptions as they orient themselves to the detail considerations they deeply need in order to become detached and relaxed.

For the intellectual type, or extrovert, this sign placement of Lilith forces forward or creates precision skills of note. For the emotional type, or introvert, the anxiety it creates about inefficiency being exposed can become detrimental to the health due to nerves, unless sufficient outlet through the vocation is found. It may take the form of a compelling medical or health consciousness that finds highly skilled outlet in one of the many health related fields. An example of this is Adele Davis, a nutritionist. In the chart of a psychic, healing or the recognition of psychic disturbances that are adversely affecting health could be the special talent in his work that distinguishes him from others in his or her field. The preoccupation with numbers may release a mathematical precision that can blossom into a highly technical vocational skill. Deep respect for technical efficiency is a noticeable signature of one who has Lilith in Virgo.

When this character magnification is not compensated for, through hobbies demanding minute application of detail that relax his anxieties on the subjective personal level, the problems incurred, from the standpoint of others, are chalked up to eccentricities or odd ego trips. Actually, they are this raw perfectionistic urge from deep within that he is unable to release that explains the irritable uneasiness, or as some might say, his sensitive spots.

Lilith in Virgo usually manifests well in this detached sign, once a profession or an area of the profession is satisfactorily found for the technical-needs release, as exemplified by astrologers Rupert Gleadow, Elbert Benjamine, and Donald Bradley. Any of the Virgo rulerships make excellent vocations if the rest of the chart permits.

People with Lilith in Virgo

Elbert Benjamine	Donald Bradley	Adelle Davis	Dwight Eisenhower
Rupert Gleadow	O. Henry		

Lilith in Libra

Lilith in Libra appears to urge obsessive interest in anything where there may be loose ends to balance out. The need to equalize inequities is a fetish. The inquisitive element is noticeably strong when there is the possibility of something being out of focus or unjust, both of which are intolerable to them. To solve even suspected disharmony, this person persists in getting all the facts. Resistance does not stop them because they have a magnified urge to resolve problems in order to bring about balance. This may be done tactfully or not according to the nature of the individual. The obvious interest these people show in other people's problems can be so flattering as to elicit the needed information.

For this reason they appear to be companionable, convivial people, which may or may not be the case. For the most part, unrestrained questioning is a signature of Lilith's placement in this balancing sign. Although curiosity may be politely couched within social chitchat or discussion seemingly for the sake of discussion, it is nevertheless there because Lilith's exaggeration in the makeup is usually well hidden in the name of conformity but is recognizable by a marked curiosity. Can you see how legal outlets, politics, or incorporating counseling as part of the vocation are socially acceptable outlets through which this drive becomes a special talent? In the life work there is peculiar ability to overcome an opponent by bringing forward his or her imbalances through taunts or questioning that literally weakens confidence, as in the case of boxer Muhammad Ali, or figuratively as in the case of an attorney crossexamining a witness in court.

There is a quality of lightness in mundane relationships that automatically discourages overly strong attachments by which one can lose perspective. This is not unlike Lilith's influence in the seventh house, where emotionally invading demands will not be tolerated for long because the only equalization possible would be the surrender of logic to feeling—unthinkable to one with the acutely liberated urges in the sign of relationships. Successful unions are made with those who are emotionally self-sustaining and open to reason.

Preference for public entertainment or social functions as opposed to the personal hospitality of close friends or family is marked, because the chance to observe the passing scene impersonally is more possible in the former than in the latter. This is not to imply a lack of consideration in the makeup, which may or may not show up elsewhere in the chart, but relationships in general are not of such emotional magnitude as to allow for bias or prejudice in favor of a particular person so that judgment is lost. They will not tolerate for long any serious inroads on their independence to mingle.

Partnerships for the sake of a helpmate in vocational efforts, or to equalize themselves whereby their identity is strengthened, may very well be the essential factor they seek in the marriage bond. There is devotion to the extent that it does not prohibit the freedom to circulate among outside impersonal interests, or to take part in the passing activities of others, where they are free to indulge in efforts to bring about balance. This is all basic to Libra promptings, but in this instance is greatly amplified by Lilith. Denial of this creates deep feelings of frustration in the relationship, and these people are apt to abruptly sever ties without any compunctions for their actions.

When outlet is found within the vocation, the creative energies naturally pour into the arts as in the case of dancer Gower Champion. This placement also gives writers and teachers of tremendous perspective, and is in one way or another the unifying element or the artistic color of the public life.

People with Lilith in Libra

Muhammad Ali	Sydney Bennett	Gower Champion	Jimmy Carter
Rudy Vallee	Booth Tarkington		

Lilith in Scorpio

With Lilith in Scorpio there is exaggerated emphasis on pride, ambition, and/or challenge. The inner need for challenge is so magnified as to make it a prime necessity within the chosen work. These people cannot withstand work where routine predominates. Instead, they must find another outlet for the overstated investigative urges. This eventually helps them set in motion the changes they determine are needed in the work atmosphere and to do away with whatever (or whoever) is obsolete. Selfishly applied, this influence brings the individual's own obsolescence down upon himself or herself. There is a deep hunger for control that is for the most part undetectable in early life. This remains so until a creative outlet or area within the vocation is found that is challenging enough to qualify for the powerful release of the individual's reform and super-perfectionistic drives in a socially acceptable manner.

There is a persistant draw to the unknown or supposed impossible. These people are valuable in research work, investigation, medical or metaphysical arts or business, where they may enjoy a delicious new set of challenges over and over within the career. Divine release from wells of submerged tension comes in the overcoming. Where there is emotional objectivity, Lilith in Scorpio gives a strong scientific bent, which can be brilliantly released.

With Lilith in Scorpio, people feel an insistent need to reach beyond themselves, to uncover hidden areas of/or attached to work that may be overcome. The extremism of Lilith in the extremist sign of Scorpio may cruelly surface to the detriment of the individual if the exaggerated personalization or overstated pride is misguided, as in the case of Richard Nixon. On the objective, impersonal level, he ended once and for all the nonrecognition of the new China in the U.N., demonstrated brilliant strategy in dealing with foreign powers and succeeded in ending active U.S. military intervention in Viet Nam. On the domestic level, he dispassionately ignored the private rights of citizens through illegal and intrusive use of the intelligence organizations under his command, bringing about his own eventual downfall. Lilith in his third house marked the extreme data hunger in his makeup, creating the incredible situation of Watergate.

These people are basically loners, contrary to outward appearances, with a near reverence for the use of strategy. They believe that growth can only come from attempting to reach beyond their stretch, so to speak, and that the only failure comes from not trying. Change is what counts, and opposing strength is respected. The personalization of the ambition is exaggerated for impressive results, as exemplified by Walt Disney, whose imagination fired an entertainment empire.

In personal areas, they need to learn to recognize that when the time arrives the real victory is in letting go; otherwise, they could suffer from self-induced emotional purging that acts as a discipline factor and that will, hopefully, leave them wiser. They need to let go of the desire for power on the mundane level. They fully understand power over others, and once a goal is set in motion it is seldom released—unless they can detach enough to gain perspective. Angles from Saturn assist in career direction because of the sense of structure and conscience it brings.

Persons with Lilith in Scorpio appear extremely controlled as a way to compensate socially, to deny the powerful tensions that drive them from within. They are not above deliberately putting on excessive weight to protect their vulnerability to emotional enslavement to another, which can be sensed in anticipated romantic relationships. There are strong (though not necessarily voiced) opinions on any subject that interests them. However, for the most part, these are held in check to avoid unnecessary exposure of the self and they may abruptly disappear when others tread too closely on their truth, as those close to these people can testify.

An early sexual awareness is intensely felt but kept to the self, lest a surfacing of something they haven't yet learned to handle is misunderstood or troublesome beyond their mien. One student made reference to this as, "making sure you can handle the dragon before unleashing it." This difference is sensed in the comparisons children automatically make to one another, which in turn are inwardly subject to denial (bottled up). It manifests in later years as a disarming magnetism that is difficult to ignore when keen interest is directed from them to another.

When desire is aroused, the concentration of feeling becomes an intensely persuasive, overly charming manner exuded over the object of interest. Under ordinary circumstances, it is not visible. Quite the contrary, it is seen on those rare occasions when this person anticipates something challenging, and then it is quite automatic. The Lilithian energy, released through the powerful desire nature of Scorpio, has a quality of fascination that draws, not unlike Neptune, but is far stronger. It is very unique to watch, and is manipulative in an effort to achieve the desired effect (probably unconscious). Magnetism seems to exude from every pore at that time. When the desire wanes, the noticeable pursuasive quality, and particularly the brilliance in the eyes, dims. This hypnotic brightening is the giveaway of Lilith in Scorpio.

Aspected to Neptune, the ability to fascinate the object of interest is magnified sexuality, as in the case of Marilyn Monroe, who had Lilith at 22 Scorpio exactly square Neptune in Leo, and also square a Moon-Jupiter conjunction (see chart 6). It did not completely penetrate the cameras but was spoken of by those who knew and worked with her as a "strange kind of pulling power she could turn on at will." In her situation, sexuality was the prime coloring of the career, the resulting magnetism of which victimized her ruthlessly most of her life. The emotional enslavement to her career ambitions (Lilith conjunct Saturn) was like a drug high to which addiction was total until finally purged. Her film career ended tragically, as did Mr. Nixon's political career. Both had Lilith square the public Moon.

In Scorpio, Lilith magnifies whatever the degree of emotional instability that lies in the makeup, which has great resource from deep wells of tension. Patricia Hearst, victimized by the S.L.A.

when she was abducted and then coerced through death threats and sexual abuse, experienced a long and violent chapter that resulted in her turning bandit. This is a particularly interesting instance, where Lilith is cuspal between two signs—in this case, leaving Libra cusping Scorpio. The following sign as possible position must be considered because of the approximate three degrees Lilith travels in one day. Because of this, it is the astrologer's burden to determine house or sign position through close observation of the individual's life events and transits over this point. The bizarre kidnapping and prolonged emotional enslavement of Patricia Hearst by a fanatic group seeking power certainly indicates a strong argument toward a 0 Scorpio Lilith position as opposed to 29 Libra.

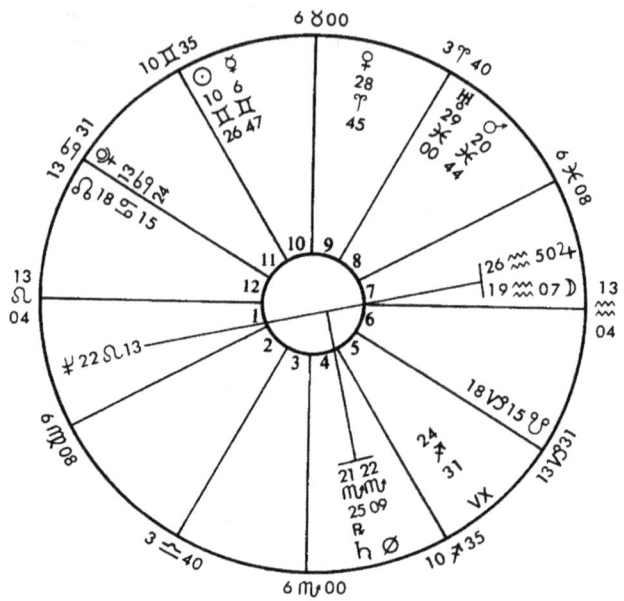

Chart 6. Marilyn Monroe, June 1, 1926, 9:30 a.m., Los Angeles, California; source: AFA Date Exchange, Rodden

When aspected with Pluto, denial of sexual expression is not uncommon. Celibacy may be preferred, forced, or accepted by choice as an answer to an unpleasant or unhealthy situation. The energy may eventually break out into strong metaphysical interest.

When desire is motivated by intellectual, creative, or social-esthetic considerations, detachment (as the impersonal) overcomes the personal, underscoring a dedicated one-pointed perseverence that will not back away from any challenge to achievement in the chosen field. In this regard there are outstanding examples such as the incredible Russian dancer, Nijinsky, and the haunting music of Sigmund Romberg. In the metaphysical field there are psychics Peter Hurkos and astrokinesis pioneer, Uri Geller. Power of one kind or another is the signature of one with Lilith in Scorpio.

People with Lilith in Scorpio

Annie Besant	Walt Disney	Uri Geller	Samuel Goldwyn
Patricia Hearst	Peter Hurkos	Christine Jorgensen	John Lennon
Marilyn Monroe	Richard Nixon	Sigmund Romberg	Pancho Villa

Lilith in Sagittarius
Lilith in Sagittarius magnifies extroverted tendencies and prods a fierce independence that is automatically guarded, resulting in fewer close personal ties. There is an adventuresome desire to constantly broaden horizons in order to insure the room needed to grow in understanding, or to roam freely, both of which bely an outer composure. A subsurface exaggerated fear of dependence is the underlying factor behind an instability, either in relationships or health; but it also accounts for greater stability in the social-universal area of larger interests and career. Independence is a fetish kept from outer view, lest it draw the kind of attention that might threaten it. This is noticeable to only a perceptive few. The deep independence need in the self, sensed in childhood, is buried in order to avoid it surfacing and coming to the attention of elders who would not understand. This becomes quite automatic in the character later on.

Partnership choices are psychologically geared toward those who are independent, effectively guaranteeing their ability to come and go as they please. They play out through the partner what they inwardly relate to but cannot openly admit for fear of denial or being misunderstood. This in no way implies a lack of devotion, but simply an unusually strong sense of adventure that seeks to continually reach for broader interests, knowledge, and fields to travel. Lilith in its fall in Sagittarius threatens serious weakness in detail perspective because of the exaggerations of the abstract. What they wish to do can be clouded or lost because of the eagerness for the joy of the hunt without an adequate roadmap of experience—unless the rest of the chart balances this urge enough to provide attention to detail.

These people are daring, reaching for the unreached in truth, or to be free to travel over the next hill if they desire, maybe for no reason other than that it is there—as Mt. Everest was to those driven to climb it. There is near reverent interest in knowledge, which exists to be picked up by their expansive antennae. Otherwise a change in direction can be immediate—whether it be the career or an area within it. By sign, Lilith describes an obsession that must find satisfaction through the vocation, avocation, or at least from a hobby, where its deviations in desire from the norm are infinitely more acceptable. In this case it would be any ninth house rulership that aids understanding or the spread of knowledge, creative independence, or simply a daring outlet that deliciously satisfies the gambler's, athlete's or traveler's desire. In most instances look for it to surface somehow, some way, as a part of the vocation and as a way to deal with abstract things as they please, the truth as they see it, or by taking chances. But an abrupt retort will quickly follow, much to the amazement of others who see only the surface poise.

If a relationship has exhausted growth potential for these people, the static condition that follows gives them a fenced-in feeling and in one way or another they will soon move on. These Lilith-sensitive spots explain many seemingingly odd ego trips that surprisingly surface if outlets are threatened. The overstated don't-fence-me-in complex will cause these people to shy and buck like a horse being put to the saddle. After all, the great soul Jupiter disposits this energy. Many entertainers have Lilith in Sagittarius, where the elements of broadcasting, promotion or travel are available. If they are in the business world they must have a certain amount of leeway to establish their own routine to come and go as they will—or they will look elsewhere.

In childhood they are not the easiest to deal with, as there is defensiveness and inner anxiety about being dependent. Feelings of limitation or too much forced dependence may seriously affect the health through Lilith in its fall in Sagittarius. If seriously curbed, the child may become ill, possibly asthmatic, if the Moon is in the sixth house in stress aspect to Mars and Lilith, or if Lilith is afflicted at 18 Sagittarius. In Sagittarius, Lilith is suspect in sugar imbalances, particularly when in stress aspect to Neptune and/or Jupiter in the sixth house is greatly afflicted.

On the personal or mundane level, there are strong anxieties for coping with things of a higher educational nature, university life, ceremonies, distant places or people. When an area is anticipated as being beyond their immediate ability to handle, these people automatically claim total disinterest. This serves to draw expectations away from the self in this area. He or she may then turn right around and pursue it, giving the appearance of instability or feigning the truth. This is not the intention at all, but one which is in reality a reactive ploy to avoid facing inadequacy, having one's motives misunderstood or running the risk of denial for a big enough opportunity.

The career may be in or take one to a foreign land, as in the case of General Douglas McArthur, writers Pearl Buck and F. Scott Fitzgerald, Jacques Cousteau and Charles Boyer, a French film actor who established himself in the United States. It may be in the clergy, as Dr. Martin Luther King, Jr. The philosophical may be the special coloring of the career, as in the case of the ballad singer Burl Ives. Last but not least is boxer Max Baer in the world of professional sports, another Sagittarian rulership.

If on the literary level, disseminating knowledge gained is a delicious release, accounting for many with this placement writing a book on whatever they feel knowledgeable in, no matter the level. They are broadcasters, advertisers or promoters, but need to first discriminate for themselves the data necessary to actualize (or factualize) what they say, or run the risk of mediocrity. Their eagerness to publish a work or spread the word quickly risks being premature, or false, if they have gambled on their inexperience, as opposed to seasoning their knowledge with more time for its fuller digestion. However, there are seasoned writers such as F. Scott Fitzgerald, Pearl Buck, and Joyce Kilmer.

The chart for the launching of the Titanic (see chart 7) shows Lilith in its fall in early Sagittarius in the third house of travel opposition the Sun, sesquisquare Neptune, conjunct Venus, ruler of the ninth (the infamous trip to New York from Southampton, England) and trine Mars. Regarding this last, the captain was determined to have as speedy a passage as possible through the

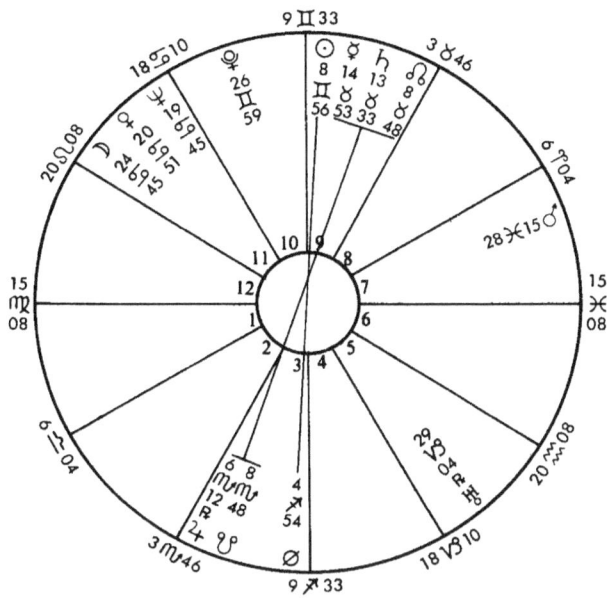

Chart 7. Launching of Titanic, May 31, 1911, 12:25 p.m., Belfast, Northern Ireland

most dangerous portion of the trip—the iceberg field. The chart ruler Mercury was conjunct Saturn in the ninth house opposition Jupiter, ruler of the fourth (the end of the matter).

To show Lilith's active part in the drama, aside from other planetary configurations, on April 14, 1912, transiting Lilith at approximately 9 Leo 11 had begun activating the midpoints of the Saturn-Mercury-Jupiter opposition, and was sesquisquare Mars, ruler of the eighth, later that day. The Titanic sank at 2:20 a.m. the following morning as the result of a violent collision with an iceberg as transiting Lilith formed a square with the Saturn-Mercury conjunctions, and transiting Mars at 5 Cancer had completed its quincunx aspect to natal Lilith opposition the Sun. The overstatement of Titanic's unsinkability under any conditions by its promoters, and the taking on of passengers before she had been fully fitted with safety gear, clearly exemplifies the exaggerated theorizing (unsinkability) and the overblown confidence in a chart containing Lilith in Sagittarius—and particularly the "blind spot" if Lilith is in a travel house. The gamble taken with this inexperienced vessel that also had less than one-half the lifeboats needed for the number of passengers on board, was the deciding factor for the unnecessary loss of lives.

Maiden Voyage: Sailed from Southhampton, England, April 10, 1912, noon. Sank at 2:20 a.m., April 15, 1912; source: library records.

People with Lilith in Sagittarius

Max Baer	Jacques Cousteau	Charles Boyer	Pearl Buck
Angela Davis	F. Scott Fitzgerald	John Glenn	Burl Ives
Joyce Kilmer	Martin L. King, Jr.	Douglas McArthur	Ronald Reagan
Van Johnson			

Lilith in Capricorn

Lilith in Capricorn describes exaggerated drive toward administrative affairs or official positions, due to a magnified sense of social duty. The need is to formalize the belief system believed to be right and to utilize to the utmost anyone capable of doing that. Failure to do so leaves a nagging feeling of having shirked responsibility. The governing complex is strong. Utilization of anything, anyone, or unpopular steps taken to complete a job, is excused in the name of duty. There is abhorence of waste and a deep awareness of time for the proper disposal of duties. Schedules are important and a fetish these people will rarely admit to.

The inner desire to govern is played down (denied) on the personal level, lest they risk a certain amount of nonconformity or expose a raw nerve that is either misunderstood or threatening on this more emotionally involved level. It is in the vocational area that this burdensome need finds release as a specific organizational, administrative, or policing talent that gives special coloring to the career, one way or another. To get into the politics of whatever they do is quite common, as in the case of concert pianist Ignace Paderewski. As a Polish statesman, he helped his country regain its independence after World War I. Or it may be in politics itself—Harry Truman, Nelson Rockefeller and George McGovern.

Exaggerated setbacks will not daunt one who has to satisfy the governing urges of Lilith in Capricorn. No matter the burden, unpopularity, or pain such a person may face from criticism, noncooperation, or personal inconvenience, shirking what is felt to be a responsibility would be even worse to this person. The Lilithian drive will not quit until an outlet is found—and then satisfied—through which to release the overstated governing sense these people feel as a moral obligation. In its highest sense, Capricorn is conscience and conscientious duty. Both of these create a compulsion for seeing failure around them as their own failure to take charge, teach, innovate, or add support to a system or politics (at whatever level) that might have avoided it, the result of which leaves them feeling strangely insecure about their position.

Franklin Roosevelt's extended hold on the presidency of the United States—unprecedented in U.S. history—caused the country to put into action certain effects that would prevent a reoccurrence. Here again is another instance of a cuspal position coming up for determination. Lilith was at 0 Aquarius on January 30, 1882, Roosevelt's birth date. Again I point out that cuspal positions (particularly 0°) must be considered to have an effect in either sign, depending upon the preponderance of weight in the chart toward one or the other. So there is a possibility that Lilith was at 29 Capricorn or 0 Aquarius.

FDR was relegated to a wheelchair existence as a result of a polio attack early in his life. His compelling urge for a political life gave rise to an intense program of rigorous self-disciplined exercises he had initiated for himself to regain at least partial use of his legs. It enabled him to overcome his disablement for all practical purposes and put an end to a "disgusting" (as he called it) waste of his life. He was in the political arena until his death in 1945. He worked under difficult physical conditions (heavy leg braces held him up in his advancing years) that would have deterred many younger people. I believe the phrase, "I want to die with my boots on," must have been coined by one with Lilith in Capricorn. In this case, to seriously consider that Roosevelt had Lilith in the last degree or minutes of Capricorn is, I believe, a reasonably valid conclusion.

Magnified desire for prestige is never completely satisfied by the usual trappings of success, if not, in fact, being denied by the lack of it, then being denied the feeling of satisfaction from it. Nor is an inferiority complex relieved by material wealth or prominence. It must result from executive or formalized work of some kind, creative excellence in the case of a writer, or a Capricorn-ruled or associated vocation. Even if they are in one of the arts, the secret desire may be to form their own company or be active in some such enterprise. They may feel compelled to do something that spells out a reality message about the conditions of the system under which they must operate, or become an authority figure in their chosen field—appearances to the contrary lest they attract those who would interfere.

Literary careers and any of the creative fields are well supported by a Capricorn Lilith, because the Lilithian influence for detachment is not denied, and is therefore not denying. These are nevertheless strong politically minded individuals who may or may not ordinarily draw public attention who are apt to lend their talent, if only indirectly, toward something that addresses the status quo. They are tireless workers and have near reverence for the ambitions of others.

For one with Lilith in Capricorn, domestic life takes second place to professional dedication. Everyday responsibilities are but a shadow of where this person's sense of achievement must come from. Depending on the rest of the chart, these people can be as loyal and supportive as anyone else, but prefer to exercise administrative power in business or other professional duties. Unreleased, it can cause depression or pessimism from nagging feelings of inferiority or irresponsibility. Family obligations ordinarily are taken care as necessary in order to get back to their professional duties, and the high level of status consciousness forbids behavior outside of accepted norms. There is no doubt that early experiences show them that this is necessary in order to keep domestic harmony, and to ensure that there is no interference by those who may suspect they are always second in importance, coming after work. They guard their ambition to officiate in important matters by drawing attention away from them, thus avoiding the unnecessary suspicions from those who would question so super a governing complex.

This social need to be in authority, hidden under conformity in the everyday areas of life, results from the habit of childhood days, when it was seen or felt as a distortion. Secret fear of denial because of this raw difference caused it to be supressed, even to themselves. It inhibited feelings of personal status through which they would later be able to judge their group worth or reputation. However, when an outlet is finally found in a vocation where there is a place for leadership, it is grasped with relish.

Rigidness in policy stamps one with Lilith in Capricorn, or parelleling the same idea, if one has Lilith closely opposition Saturn from the eighth house, as had Angela Davis (see chart 4). If certain politics, policies, or systems are considered to be impractical, wasteful, or without proper discipline and direction, there can be exaggerated efforts to defeat them or to support the formalization of others. This was the case with Angela Davis, who finally joined the Communist Party, resulting in the highly publicized loss of her prestigious teaching position at a California university. Self-serving action or giving away to the emotional factor causes situations that force one with Lilith in Capricorn, or in this case, opposition Saturn, to knuckle under to a rigid authority figure, suffer a bad reputation, or in severe instances, be jailed, as she was.

In the entertainment field Johnny Carson's amazing fortitude, excellent production sense, and loyalty to a grueling schedule accounted for the long-standing success of his nightly television show. In Capricorn, Lilith attested to his outstanding executive talent and genius for delegating duties to responsible people. Carol Burnett's talent in the same field is a close parallel. Carson admitted that his record of domestic failures was, for the greater part, due to his professional dedication.

In the arts these people can rise to excellence because of their rigid sense of self-discipline, perfect sense of timing, and capacity for hard work. The musical field has Serge Kousevitsky, symphony conductor; Andres Segovia, guitarist; and Ignace Paderewski, concert pianist. In the literary field is William Faulkner.

People with Lilith in Capricorn

Carol Burnett	Johnny Carson	Willi m Faulkner	Serg Kousevitsky
Karl Krafft	George McGovern	Ignace Paderewski	Nelson Rockefeller
Andres Segovia	Harry Truman		

Lilith in Aquarius
In Aquarius, Lilith gives an exaggerated orientation to the future, resulting in a liberal viewpoint and humanitarian ideas for today. Everything must serve a practical purpose toward the future, which they relate to more than the present. They are focused on progressive ideas rather than contemporary ones, and if something does not serve that end, it is discarded. It is the promise of tomorrow that is important! As something envisioned becomes part of the present, no longer a future promise, interest is apt to be lost. The function of Lilith in Aquarius has been satisfied, and a new concept will take its place on the horizon of this person's vision of the future. These people are never really a part of the contemporary scene, despite appearances, but are always living in the future.

The world of unusual or progressive ideas for the future is their playground, and material objects merely serve as a means to assist in crystallizing their inventive, progressive vision. This is of course acute or somewhat modified according to the rest of the chart, and is outwardly compelling if in aspect with Jupiter, Pluto, or Neptune, and more conservative if with Saturn. If in aspect with Uranus, it can result in an inventor or astrologer par excellance. Aspected to Uranus it implies genius. People with Lilith in Aquarius are kind and considerate of others, but only insofar as it does not impinge on their freedom. If angular, this Lilith position creates an eccentricity that causes them to be considered special, or be misunderstood.

They can maintain a composure that belies the nervous pull of this unusual future orientation. There exists an underlying anxiety in the makeup, lest progress or the freedom urges be thwarted or somehow denied, even becoming suspicious of anything that might suggest it. These people will not long tolerate circumstances that would make tomorrow's world but a distant, likely unreachable goal. Marriage may be delayed for this reason, because these people do not easily give up their freedom. They believe in indepence for its own sake, but at times find themselves carrying the burden of another person—but in a different way. By avoiding marriage, for example, these people may inherit the burden of caring for a parent.

The marked freedom urges and unconventional ideas are not outwardly apparent because these people learn to conform during their childhood years lest they be considered an oddity by their playmates and thus be denied friendships. The early denial makes this characteristic sink deeply beneath the surface only to later become exaggerated in importance. Blessed relief is usually found through the vocation, where eccentricities, interest in the sciences of tomorrow and occult or inventive ideas can be accepted when applied for the public good or in a service occupation. Drawing the least attention to it (which is quite automatic in adult life) guards against the interference they are unsure they can handle. This accounts for some of the illusiveness or secretiveness of these people. The practicing astrologer with this position is particularly gifted.

When manifesting negatively at the private level, and particularly when in strong aspect to Jupiter, which feeds the exaggeration, it can involve a situation concerning "the other woman" or being the third person in a triangle. In the eleventh house or aspected to its ruler, Lilith can describe a free-love attitude, or an astrological orientation, or both. The emphasis on unconventional involvements accounts for a secrecy many are unaware of, are reminiscent of Aquarius's ruler, Uranus, exalted in Scorpio.

Preference for detached as opposed to attached relationships stamps one with Lilith in Aquarius. Anxieties mount if they suspect any possessive ploys (consciously or not) that indicate the beginnings of any emotional or overly-personal involvements. They may suddenly blurt out the uselessness of it (self-protection) to the amazement of others, particularly if they are spotting the trend before the other person even thinks of it.

They are so strong in their determination that their freedom is never in danger of being hampered, and this can distort their judgment during budding personal relationships. This can cause the very loss of friendship they enjoy, need, and revere.

This is especially so if Lilith is dynamically aspecting Uranus or Uranus has a strong influence in the chart. The intuitive suspicion, when suddenly voiced, creates a feeling of total surprise in others—disbelief and resentment that they are suddenly being judged almost as if having contemplated a criminal action.

Aquarians with Lilith in Aquarius are eccentric. There is nothing contemporary about these people. They belong to the future. The live the hope of a better world, and in charts that are intellectually or creatively motivated, they contribute something toward making that vision a reality.

Lilith in Aquarius is associated with astrologers and those whose vocations foster inventive, technological, or humanitarian ideas. Some examples are: Carl Jung, Winston Churchill, William Herschell (discovered Uranus), William Jennings Bryant, and Walter P. Chrysler. George Wallace, the controversial former governor of Alabama, understood the value of shock-tactics and was well known for his upsetting, unvarnished views.

In a creative chart Lilith in Aquarius magnifies musical talent, giving geniuses such as Leonard Bernstein, George Gershwin, George M. Cohen, and the exquisite Russian dancer, Anna Pavlova. To attain their goals these people are capable (depending on the rest of the chart) of great fortitude, patience, and a rigid self-discipline in line with the Aquarian sub-ruler Saturn's influence.

People with Lilith in Aquarius

Alice Bailey	Leonard Bernstein	Walter P. Chrysler	George M. Cohen
Moisha Dayan	George Gershwin	William Herschell	L. Edward Johndro
Carl Jung	Anna Pavlova	Ringo Starr	William J. Bryant

Lilith in Pisces

Lilith in Pisces is a well of etheric energy from which springs extraordinary imagination, the ability to work with intangibles, a mystical awareness, and musical or other Neptunian drives, urges, or phobias. Here is the need to release energy through psychic or related fields, through work with the handicapped or those who are discriminated against or confined, and in sound, lighting, videography, film, or photography. They work well with vibration—monitoring soundwaves through oscilloscopes, or working with devices such as sound pressure meters and frequency counters used in designing sound systems. They have particularly sensitive hearing.

There is exaggerated sensitivity to the delicate intangibles in life, creating strong introversion when such release is consistently denied. Consider the fishes of Pisces, one aware of the material world, and the other equally aware of the etheric one. Now see each awareness magnified by Lilith for either creative release or negative escapism. Lilith overstates the esthetics, ideals, and love orientation that are already strong in the nature of Pisces, making these people work well with impressionism, illusions, music, design or anything that has a flowing quality. They are apt to have some degree of clairvoyance or clairaudience. This is apparent to only a close few who can recognize the deep inner attunement to kirlian realities when positive, or to fantasies when negative.

The world of reflection, illusion, rhythm, color or lights needs to be somehow released within the vocation, or at least through a hobby. The denial of it creates self-undoing because the energy buildup encourages disorientation. In the self-centered person, or where the emotional nature is undisciplined, the visionary quality can become distorted, as when one is looking at something under water and not making allowances for the difference in dimension: in this case, distortion between what these people see and what they think they see. When positive, the products of a highly creative imagination can be reflected in the arts and in professions such as acting, dancing, staging, or one of the metaphysical disciplines; in other words, wherever feelings or impressions are reflected, worked with or channeled. Such unusual talent may be channeled through any work that deals with the reflective processes, where the world of light and shadow is used such as in television and film. If the rest of the chart is supportive, it may bring work dealing with the reflective ethers themselves, as in psychic or other occult fields. This sensitivity can also be released through delicately artistic needlework, interior decorating, fashion design, and hospital volunteer work. The unusual talent for elevating the lives of the handicapped was particularly demonstrated by Helen Keller in her memorable work with the blind.

Lilithian energy manifests positively only as a distinctly impersonal force; in other words, beyond self-considerations, as opposed to Luna's distinctly personal one. With the energy blocked on selfish, emotional, and materialistic levels, Lilith here denies gratification; but within the detachment of service, the arts, or the mind, Lilith is a significator of strong talent.

These urges are held deeply within since childhood, where these people denied (or the urges were otherwise repressed) their sensitivity to unknown factors. They deny their natural psychic awareness in order to avoid being misunderstood or being considered strange, or from a fear of being unable to handle the Lilith influence. There is an unusually acute dream state that most people keep to themselves because of the apparent oddness of it in comparison to others.

These people can be unbelievably naive about life, and particularly about love, which to them is the essence of life's meaning, opening them to painful, even tragic, disillusionment as in the life of early film actress Jean Harlow, a suicide at 26. They do not suffer the usual pains of disillusionment in love; they feel destroyed and hurt beyond a depth difficult to imagine. Lilith in Leo might say, "The play is the thing." Lilith in Pisces would say, "The dream's the thing." These people literally feel the concrete existence of whatever they believe in. The fantasy world or the imaginings of childhood never quite leave them, accounting for the charming lack of sophistication that surrounds many of these people and the unreal situations they can attract.

The creative people among this group make natural dancers, singers, or musicians. The magnified etheric quality of their nature can create the fertile imaginative genius to reproduce the sights, sounds, and feelings of higher worlds, as Russian ballet dancer and choreographer Leonide Massine superbly portrayed both on stage and in films. Other people with Lilith in Pisces are opera singer Joan Sutherland and Russian composer Igor Stravinsky, who greatly influenced the course of contemporary music.

The world of "let's pretend" is a favorite, and it has produced such sensitive film stars as Irene Dunne and Charlie Chaplin, silent film star and a master of impressions, with a genius for pantomime.

Where the impressionability is channeled through intellectual objectivity, as in the case of film star Will Rogers who had Lilith trine his Scorpio Sun, Lilith in Pisces can release as a gentle but teasing cynicism, applied through the relaxing ploy of comedy. The use of laughter protects these individuals from reactions they prefer to avoid; in other words, saying what they think but giving the illusion that it said itself.

The endless imagination and secret preoccupation with idealism and love brings eventual disillusionment if the energy is not channeled through some specialized area in their work, causing the buildup of sensitivity to erupt as a fantasy they live. These people refuse, more and more, to see things as they really are, preferring to see them as they imagine them to be, like some Utopian dream. They prefer the lulling comfort of an imagined security rather than putting an end to an obvious deception or an unstable situation in which they are unfairly taken advantage of and to which others usually alert them. They can be sacrificial beyond belief in order to satisfy their ideal. The sweet dream of illusion is by far the more real situation to them, and it is reality that seems like a dream. They can sidestep a problem for a time by simply not believing there is a problem, in order to protect their illusion. Lilith's distortion makes it this person's reality, and thus his or her Achilles Heel. The disillusionment that Lilith causes on the emotional level eventually acts as an emotionally maturing factor. Parallel this to Saturn's disciplines to mature one on the material level, both acting as necessary controls and limitations.

Compassion, perception and a charming gentleness are noted in the mature types; emotional naivete and procrastination are noted in the negative types. Soft aspects from Saturn are strongly stabilizing for greater realistic direction, whereas Jupiter aspects enlarge the already over-proportioned sensitivity to even greater heights. Mars and Neptune are particularly potent in soft or hard aspect.

These are not basically earth-bound spirits, but ones who feel an inner kinship with the auric world that enfolds the form world. It belies their protective outer facade of earthier interest. The deep sensitivity to superphysical influences was amply demonstrated by Edgar Cayce. Jerry Brown, former California governor who was often called the "political mystic," significantly colored his early career with mystical remarks of man's unity with all life and metaphysical references, as opposed to the usual formal religious beliefs, having renounced the world for four years to live in a Buddhist monastery. He demonstrated his affinity to hold onto a dream long after it ceased to exist, to the point of embarrasment to his party and followers, maintaining intense campaigning long after he was clearly defeated in the presidential primaries of 1976.

People with Lilith in Pisces

JerryBrown	Edgar Cayce	Charlie Chaplin	Irene Dunne
Jean Harlow	George Harrison	Helen Keller	Leonide Massine
Will Rogers	Igor Stravinsky	Joan Sutherland	Glen Campbell

Chapter 4

Lilith Through the Houses

When evaluating Lilith in the houses, it is well to keep in mind that wherever Lilith is located, it is one's own emotional immaturity or naivete; in other words, shallow expectations, that negate good judgment and create distortion. It is where the sophistication of impersonality, hopefully gained through flat denials of self-centered juvenile expectations, is of prime necessity to be introduced into the character. This is in order to successfully overcome outgrown dependencies (childish carryovers), that though comfortable enough, are contrary to further emotional maturity.

In effect, depersonalization within the astrological houses are what Lilith is all about. It is where personality problems are spotlighted on superficial or self-centered levels. It is where individuals must learn to overcome the controlling influences of the house or of their own lower nature that retards their creative mental or spiritual development. In short, this is where people are constantly faced on the mundane level with having to grow up emotionally. Sound cold? Probably so. Maybe this is why Lilith has such a negative reputation. We all hate to let go of our "teddy bears" in one area or another even though we do not see these as naive expectations until a shocking, demeaning, or at least a surprising Lilith experience teaches us how naive we really are. To whatever extent one lacks the ability to be objective (and we all are to some degree), Lilith will be the eroding factor that seriously prompts a higher application of the mind and spirit.

Where Lilith is located is where individuals will encounter the reflections of their own negative emotionalism. It is pictured through situations or other people that force a certain amount of objectivity, if only out of self-defense, in order to cope with the circumstances or the person of that house. Like Saturn, Lilith can leave individuals embittered or not, depending upon the rest of the chart. However, it will certainly leave them more aware of the emotional dependencies that are at the bottom of their inability to cope in matters related to that particularly house.

The overall growth from these usually early experiences appears to be relatively good in a large majority of the charts studied. This is probably because through forced depersonalization—from whatever the circumstances—came a fuller use of the intellect, creativity, or independence. Through concentration on higher interests or goals, emotional order is created in the house Lilith occupies. For the strongly mental or creative types this can come about relatively smoothly.

Lilith rules the intellectual soul (higher instincts), and only represents distortions when there is subjective personalization, selfishness, or passivity in the house it motivates. Robert Hand says, "Luna represents the irrational part of the mind that is largely controlled by emotions." I have found, in comparing our first satellite to the second, that it is Lilith that represents the rational part of the mind and is denied for anything but the rational. As Saturn (Lilith's parallel) disciplines improperly organized activity into order or denies it totally, so too does Lilith within the desire nature. As Saturn is absolute, Lilith is extreme. One of the most noticeable points of the higher side of Lilith is the amazing inspiration this individual can eventually be to others where the house and/or sign of Lilith is concerned. These people can literally intuit solutions related to the sign or house, or be productive far beyond their expectations.

Lilith's daily mean motion from $3°$ to $3°2'$ parallels the Uranus-Pluto midpoint travel of $3'2''$, a 3-2 ratio. In like manner of Uranus-Pluto connections, Lilith's action consistently appears to be either incredibly progressive and creative, or emotionally unpredictable and unnerving. The benefit of these frustrations is that through painful experience you will never again be the same emotionally. You may be a little sadder, but hopefully a little wiser. Call it sophistication. Call it Lilith. Whether this leaves you with resentment will depend upon you and your ability to let go of self-importance and develop a sense of humor about yourself. Believe me, where there is Lilith you need a sense of humor, even if it is only a wry one at first.

Negative effects come from Lilith when we live in our lower nature at the Lilith point, and positive effects that are a distinct blessing come when we live in our higher nature. These positive releases are activated only within attitudes or interests through which we can impersonally express ourselves or challenge our minds or the imagination, or within the vocation. Lilith is positive within areas that circumvent the personal ego or the desire nature for the work to be done or the service performed.

Angular in a chart or otherwise prominent, Lilith gives a fascinating quality not unlike a Neptune effect. It brings an illusive quality to a house that, like Neptune, will erode or confuse the negative and elevate to enlightenment the positive or selfless motivation.

Lilith in the First House
To a certain extent Lilith in the first house parallels Lilith in Aries because the natural background ruler of this house is Mars. The difference is that in Aries, Lilith is already set in the character, whereas in the first house it is in the stage of becoming a part of the character. It deeply influences the physical disposition, early environment, and method of self-projection. Self-consciousness and the personal element are unusually strong because Lilith magnifies whatever it touches on whatever level, positive or negative. Thus, in the first, Lilith creates an inexhaustible drive for personal identity because these people feel recognition is denied. In this house, Lilith means that personal detachment and objectivity, as opposed to the usual subjective behaviorial and environmental influences be developed as an integral part of the personality. The impersonal approach to life is eventually forced upon these people because they are unable to in any other way develop a secure sense of self-identity. Lilith is impersonal and demands a depersonalization in this one's approach to life, or it creates a frustrating sense of facelessness that accounts for an incredible inferiority complex or seemingly cold behavior, almost as if devoid of feeling.

From early on, these people experience a nagging inner sense of personal denial when projecting themselves along the usual day-to-day outlets for the mundane gratifications that are naturally subject to the approval or disapproval of others. They feel overlooked and unappreciated. There is nothing subjective about Lilith; indeed, quite the opposite is true. A satisfying sense of identity is gained only by projecting the self through the intellect, the creative imagination, or eventually, via what is done vocationally. Here, self-projection is necessarily more impersonal, and these people feel barren and inferior even though this is carefully hidden. Lilith is pure denial on superficial levels or within selfish motivation, and is the significator, the denial, in instances of physical handicap or environmental limitation.

In youth, these people feel greatly overshadowed by the personalities of others, inadequate or strangely different, resulting in deeply rooted feelings of inferiority, particularly about their personal appearance. Frustrations in ordinary everyday relationships are not uncommon, particularly during these early years. Whether or not it is true, they feel cancelled out by others, particularly when projecting themselves for personal/emotional advantage or approval. Some may compensate for the frustration through a deliberately asserted independence in order to draw attention to themselves. Usually it is the wrong kind of attention they may finally attract, ending with just another frustration, or being disciplined rather than gratified. It may erupt in an action, sometimes to them, but mostly from them, that appears surprisingly out of character or self-defeating. There are some who may, on the other hand, simply draw into themselves, appearing mysterious or special until they can find an outlet for self-expression through something they do rather than through themselves personally.

There is nothing about Lilith that satisfies superficial personal desires when in the first house. It brings no satisfying existence to these people until the higher things of the mind are found, the creative spirit expressed, or a career through which the higher social needs they finally recognize they have can be released and identified. Within these areas they can beautifully depersonalize and become truly impressive personalities. Depersonalization is what they must develop through interests outside of themselves in order to gain the personal objectivity Lilith demands in the first house. Of course, the extent of success differs with each individual chart.

The intellectual or strongly positive types have more natural ability to be detached, or at least to be more emotionally independent, and thus flow more readily with Lilith in the first. There are also those among the subjective types who have Uranus strong enough in their charts to finally develop an "I don't care" attitude. They will lose themselves in a creative area or hobby, or a mental, social, or technical interest through which they discover personal satisfactions and eventually their broader identity through achievement. This may also come through a natural or deliberate bookishness, which satisfies the strong intellectual sense. It could also come from simply learning to take a philosophic approach in personal matters.

Any one of these extroverted avenues seeds a less subjective and more detached approach to life that promotes greater maturity. This form of self-projection leaves people with this placement less subject to direct personal approval, but more subject to approval for a special talent which Lilith then brightly focuses. When LIlith is positive on the personal level, it greatly furthers magnetism and creative talent. Lilith's specialized energy is blocked from a positive outlet only when negated within the emotional static of superficial desires, becoming denying, frustrating, or repressing. Subjectivity, sentiment, and emotionalism are Luna's domain, as Luna rules the emotional soul. It is Lilith that rules the intellectual soul and is anathema to human weakness.

When these people finally depersonalize, or in other words become emotionally liberated from themselves (forget about themselves), by viewing life through more objective eyes, strong confidence and a fascinating quality of true specialness arises. It makes them difficult to overlook. As Lilith frustrates personality on selfish levels, it exaggerates personal charisma within mental-creative interests, creating a disarming charm and noticeable power of attraction. Lilith elevates on objective levels. It then brings to this kind of personality an exuberance that is so automatically attention-drawing as to appear flirtatious or coquettish, even though this is far from the intention. They can become intently absorbed in an object of interest or someone they meet, actually trying to penetrate the superficial personality, and others recognize this from the specialized gaze that is focused on them, particularly when of the opposite gender. A disarming curiosity is exuded as they eagerly seek to "know" others. Parallel this with Lilith in Aries.

Personality is so pronounced as to be a key factor in the vocation, and they become known personalities in their chosen career field. They can be inspiring instructors and quite charismatic as leaders. These are one-of-a-kind people. They are unique. They are pathfinders. At the very least, there are no "ordinary" types among those with Lilith in the first house.

In the event that objectivity is difficult or impossible to maintain in the personal areas of life because of many subjective planets or Sun, there are those who will prefer to go anywhere or do anything only in pairs or as part of a group. They will surround the self with others selves in order to have a self. Do you see the constant impersonal self-projection this makes possible?

The emotional inferiority complex they feel in everyday activities is very real where relationships are concerned, contrary to outer appearances, whereas on impersonal levels where detachment is possible, they come alive in a way that can only be described as fascinating.

Aside from finding satisfaction through literary, esthetic, or career achievement, there are those with subjective charts who may nevertheless still resent having had to find personal fulfillment this way instead of through marriage. There can remain a haunting disatisfaction for a mate they feel has disappointed them, or this may come from the mate who feels left out of so important and fulfilling a part of their lives. Lilith does not promise ease on personal/emotional levels, no matter the higher development. It is only through the higher level that they can gain the objectivity to successfully deal with it. Depending on the extent of introversion in the chart, a resentful independence may plague a marriage until they can find a creative rapport with a mate through an interest that can be shared. They may come together by sincerely trying to understand each other and then to respect and accept their individual differences.

Home, family, and motherhood/fatherhood are not sufficiently satisfying when Lilith is in the first house. These people are usually career oriented as well as literary, artistic, or socially-minded. One woman with Lilith and the Moon conjunct in the first house simply solved the dilemma by adopting a separate name (identity) for her business personality.

Lilith in the Second House

In the second house, Lilith demands things and activities that enrich the mind and spirit, and there are unusually strong security needs from childhood on. It is not as much for material gain as it is for an emotional security that these people always feel a haunting lack of in ordinary relationships. For this reason, in early in life they tend to become overly attached to one particular person; many times it is a sibling. There are frustrations and eventual denial through such a dependency, which only serves to block what they really need—a sense of self worth—until they look for more than mere superficial emotional security through another. They must build this for themselves through higher esthetic desires that finally satisfy from within. When the crutch relationship is finally lost they realize how alone they are.

Lilith creates a compelling inner need for the objective values of the mind, the imagination, or the creative spirit to be brought out in order to give needed substance and direction to this one's further emotional maturing and sense of personal value to others, not to mention to self. The lack of this is deeply felt as a personal inability to attract affection. Without the development of impersonal desires, they lack personality completion and thus personal stabilization and a healthy self-evaluation, which is insidiously self-defeating—appearances aside.

For the mental, artistic, mystical, or philosophical type, self-worth and personal sustainment through emotionally impersonal values are developed earlier. Creative types would more naturally consider their talents and their knowledge as the riches that give meaning to life and self-worth. They devote effort to personal development and the resulting accomplishments rather than on acquiring things, and value artistic things that inspire, music, literature, education, and faith in God. Nothing less will ever be enough to mature and thereby stabilize the personality by which he can live through himself instead of through another.

For the materialistic or selfishly emotional type, or one who for the wrong reasons is still clinging to sentimental or childhood values, sexual prowess, or things that insure or secure love due to societal programming, deeply rooted insecurity anxiety remains for a longer time as the psychological basis of a painful inferiority complex. Spiritual values, creative or literary talents, or interests through which the intuition or the imagination may flower, or a profession that provides a specialized outlet for these things can set these people free from exaggerated emotional dependency when Lilith is in the second house.

No matter how much these people may eventually own, or their devotion in emotional relationships, it is never quite enough to make them happy. They always feel somehow poor, or anticipate rejection before it, in fact, occurs, creating the kind of negative sensitivity that is self-limiting. This often leads them to reject someone rather than chance being rejected. Guarded insecurities are absorbed until one day they are desperately voiced to the surprise of someone who was completely unaware that the insecurities existed. The undiscovered higher values that seek to rise in these people's consciousness are what is behind the inner unrest or outer problems that continually make them feel insecure. It results in an unhealthy dependence on either what is owned or the need to compromise emotional security from outside the self. In their early lives, these people feel trapped because ordinary things do not give them freedom, or the feeling of freedom, that security would ordinarily symbolize. They are often accused of hiding their light under a bushel.

They certainly will not lack for material necessities (if not more) because the exaggerated security instinct creates enough conservatism (or fear) to motivate them, personal feelings aside. In what then are they poor? What is lacking? When negative (selfishly oriented), it is the satisfaction they never feel when they finally get what they want, going on and on down this empty corridor of superficial desire that never quiets them—thus an insecurity complex. The psychological unrest simply comes from a values system that is too shallow for them, and so they feel shallow. There are sudden cries for affection and devotion to make them feel they count in life. Lilith frustrates these naive (for them) expectancies.

The type of security one instinctively seeks is based on the things or matters to which one relates. When ordinary things prove empty, as they surely will when Lilith is in the second house, then logically there is something wrong with the whole set of values. Obviously they are relating to the wrong things or for the wrong reasons. They will not find gold in a coal mine, just as surely as they will not find mental or spiritual enrichment through materialistic attitudes. The objective and impersonal values of the intellect and creative levels that are rich in them are from where their particular maturity and freedom must come. These are their real needs rather than the material ones that only keep them enslaved to an inconstant security from outside rather than from within. The victory is in the letting go. Stop the chase for subjective things or relationships, and begin the search for spiritual understanding or for intellectual or artistic outlets. By doing this, their woefully lacking emotional perspectives can be changed because this is what in essence they really hungers for, consciously or not. When they finally begin to equate their personal worth with achievement, spiritual development, or growth in a literary or creative field, the deep feelings of insecurity seem to melt away.

Lilith directs the desire nature to guidance by the mind or the inner spirit to awaken mental/creative desire and focus, and through it, emotional adulthood. Deep appreciation of fine music, opera, the arts, and all things beautiful can be cultivated, through which feeling is then channeled into a higher outlet. Music studies are very good, as they guide the emotional factor into nonpersonal applications of feeling. There lies in this person a strong sense of the beautiful and the worth of the individual. It is crying for development once the channels have been cleared of emotional static.

For these people, impersonal interests stabilize the personality beautifully. Detachment stabilizes attachment. Selflessness releases them to a greater feeling of personal worth, gained absolutely no other way when Lilith is in the second house. Certainly there will be times when they fall back into nagging insecurity anxieties during times of materialistic orientation due to pressures or selfish ambition. Nevertheless, they can regain themselves through renewed efforts along creative lines, selflessness, or prayerful meditation. Only selfishness, ego trips, or foolish ideals create Lilithian denials. There is nothing subjective about Lilith energy that can long be tolerated. For this, it is denial with a capital D. It is Luna that is the ruler of the emotional soul. Lilith rules the intellectual soul and magnifies the talents of the mind and creative imagination to translate feeling into inspiration. Lilith exaggerates to awareness an inner beauty from faith in a universal wisdom; otherwise a feeling of futility remains. The command is clearly made for the higher approach to worldly things.

When positive, Lilith brings to these individuals an impressive confidence that literally shines from them and inspires, resulting in support, respect, appreciation from others, and an earning power that will sustain their material needs. It will come automatically by ratio to their higher interests, spiritual growth, and impersonally helpful efforts where others are concerned. The mistake is to aim for esthetic satisfactions and outer laurels that in the end only deter them from their goals and cause them to fall back into the old denials. Without such motivation, these people are among the most emotionally dependent and insecure souls you will ever meet, as those close to them can verify. Suffice it to say that where Lilith is found by house position it is one's own immaturity or shallow expectations (naivete) that weakens judgment, and where sophisticatton strengthens it.

The second house represents a great deal more than just the individual's worldy riches. It represents what comes from his or her particular enrichment. In this case, it is books, music, art, education, writing, research, occult knowledge, selflessness; or a professional dedication in service. These people must come to the realization that material gain is purposeful, but it is not the purpose itself. People with a second house Lilith may put great store on their libraries, studies, creations, art objects, or faith. Indeed, they may have a wall filled with framed credits, honors, pictures of admired and accomplished people, first editions, autographed books, or framed letters. If the truth be known, they more often identify with these than they do with home and family.

More often than not these people have natural musical or speaking ability. The singers and lecturers among them have an unusually fascinating quality in their voices. Those who investigate metaphysics soon learn that thoughts and the spoken word are indeed concretely real in their particular reality, the world of mind. They learn that virtues are very real possessions (contrary to materialistic thought) that act as a refinement and enrichment of the soul, and that music and art are concrete products of the spirit. As Lilith magnifies the negative, it magnifies the positive, exaggerating talents and faith through concentration on beauty and knowledge. It brings to them a powerful quality of self-sustainment about themselves that is amazing and inspiring to others. Although some of these people may appear less rich in the goods of the world, they have that sense of fullness that may mystify others who judge only by material wealth.

Lilith in the Third House
People with Lilith in the third house can be among the most intuitive and intelligent among us. They have unusually fine minds and creative imaginations. However, this is realized only on the highest level when the mind is subjected to service or things creative, or once they have learned to depersonalize their thinking. This is a must, as Lilith demands impersonal attitudes in order to release positive mental talent. There is a strange kind of logic otherwise, that incredibly centers around the emotions or personal biases because of the exaggerated susceptibility to the desire nature when subjective or self-conscious.

When personal ego (theirs or another's) dominates their thoughts or invades work projects, or they are dealing with people with whom they feel strong emotional undercurrents (which incidentally the other person may be totally unaware of), their mental processes become frustrated. The emotions then become totally involved, logical processes are blocked, and they take everything personally. They then either lose track of the subject, forget words or stumble over them, or turn a subject suddenly around into a defense of themselves, much to the amazement of others. Depending on the chart, they may compensate in other ways such as suddenly proclaiming disinterest in the entire subject, or likely as not, simply change it, become defensively rude, irritatingly evasive, or just give up in silence.

On Lilith's lower level there is unreasoning, or blind, fear of facing the issues of Lilith's house placement, which in this case is the need for development of the creative scope of mental expression. The crucial need is for objectivity and interest only in the subject matter and not on personalities. The need is for detachment, which is the key for turning Lilith into a creatively beneficial influence. The third house rules concrete thought, the intellect, and the ability to communicate. Lilith as the impersonal principle is anathema to human weakness; therefore, with Lilith in the third house, unless these people can remain sufficiently detached from ego involvements they find it impossible to concentrate, rendering communication barren of its intended message.

Wherever Lilith is located is where naivete or emotional insecurity creates a serious lack of perspective and childlike expectancies, which are the native's self-undoing. In the third, it then creates frustration in learning, inability to communicate, or deal with third house matters or persons effectively. It is where one must work to develop impartiality; otherwise there is total loss of concentration or any number of events that make learning more difficult or frustrate the literary life.

When superficially or selfishly oriented (consciously or not), these people anticipate rejection or being misunderstood, not believed, or intellectually outclassed. This creates defensive anxieties about their inadequacy to communicate and a deeply rooted inferiority complex concerning their intelligence; this can affect the speech. It is amazing to see these people do exceptionally well in degree studies as preparation for a profession; however, in learning for personal pleasure or enrichment, even letter writing, they can feel beaten before they start.

Lilith's positive effects are felt only within interests that impersonally challenge the mind or imagination, or do the same within the vocation. Effects are positive within attitudes that circumvent the personal ego or desire nature for the work to be done or service to be performed. Those with Lilith in the third deeply desire and need the objectivity such a climate fosters in order to stay above the emotional factor that limits their perspective and causes their reasoning to be muddled. With a naturally mentally-oriented person, intellectual detachment is more readily achieved. However, these people feel acutely out of place or become ineffective, as if they are strangely removed, when personalities enter into their work or conversation; at times they're unsure they're even being heard. If the ego is involved, they may (without realizing it) slip into a preoccupation with their own opinions or become repetitious in order to get a subject back on the track. It is almost impossible for them to concentrate under negative influences, because of their emotional susceptibility. There is nothing subjective about Lilith, so they are easily frustrated. When objectivity is denied, Lilith denies. This is opposed to the strictly logical professional or creative approach that clears their fine minds to advise, teach, write, or express meaningfully. In fact, they may find themselves in possession of some startling talents like precognition, clairvoyance, or a gift for writing that comes through inspiration. Lilith is extreme either way, and its action is not unlike the Uranus-Pluto midpoint.

On Lilith's lower fear level there can be manuscript losses, plagiarism, problems with the press (Richard Nixon), difficulties with siblings or neighbors, and speech problems. No matter the talent, success in writing or having work published is somehow blocked if the individual is negative (tension-ridden) about whether it will be well accepted rather than having concern for the validity or excellence of the material for its own sake. On the higher side, Lilith magnifies the ability to inspire others with literary ambition. They will give of themselves unstintingly in their assistance and can be extremely supportive because there is near reverence for literary talent.

These people can be the most provocative of speakers with fascinating powers of suggestion. Boxer Muhammed Ali was able to use provocative suggestions of defeat in dealing with an opponent before a bout; he systematically applied psychological pressure. One of the most effective lecturers I have heard has Lilith in the third house conjunct Venus and Jupiter in Gemini and square an angular Mars conjunct Neptune. She can present her subject with complete assurance and professionalism even while placidly enjoying a small cigar. She does not miss a chance to bring in scolding insights on human frailty through thought-provoking asides. They are suprisingly well received because of the unique talent Lilith gives for being impersonally personal, caring but uninvolved. A well aspected third house Lilith with strong air positions may indicate one who starts talking at an unusually early age, and possibly speaking in complete sentences by age one.

These people can be invaluable in any of the communication fields as, for example, travel agents or executive assistants, or in the media. They need to be independent thinkers and will be anything but mediocre when the concentration is on the work and not on themselves. In radio or television they can be particularly talented for putting all the different facets of a show together or editing it for tape. They seem to be on top of everything with the greatest of ease. In highly positive charts and with Aquarius rising or a heavy air stellium, early communication problems or an intellectual inferiority complex appears to be overcome earlier in life. This is due to the natural detachment in the character that asserts itself as these people mature or successfully move away from those who have an emotional affect on them. It may even challenge them to greater heights for having lived the frustration, once they learn how to remain impersonal when getting their ideas across. When the influence is negative, they should deter their emotions by saying nothing or simply walk away rather than appear foolish.

Emotions can interfere with vocal expression to such an extent as to cause slurred speech or stuttering. There is excellent reasoning power when the native finally depersonalizes his or her thinking. Otherwise, it is as though these people must work with extreme difficulty to get each word out. The words seem to, almost hysterically, pile up in the mind too fast for the individual to sort them out. This can result in an inability to speak, garbled words, or speech that sounds like a needle slowing down on a phonograph record. Several of these people have told me they feel at times as if their tongues were too large for their mouths, making it impossible for them to get words out. When they are very tired, you may notice slurred speech, almost as if intoxicated. The best advice at times like this is for these people to let it go until enough time has passed to regain their perspective.

We know that communication is crucial to relationships. Where there are marital problems, look for Lilith in the third house as the possible crux of misunderstandings. A third party, such as a counselor, may be able to create the impartial atmosphere that is needed through which these people can express their problems. Hopefully, they will come to realize that it is their own unreasoning fear and self-centered preoccupation that negates communication between themselves and others.

Ordinarily many of these people find solace in reading to keep their minds clear, or to clear it. Meditation is excellent for developing concentration because when emotions are stilled, they can mentally roam through the myriad details of an experience or conversation to gain perspective on it. At times like this their mental processes can travel into the higher realms of the imagination, where they receive startling ideas or clear impressions of knowledge. Many psychic or metaphysical readers have this placement.

It is not uncommon to find that somone with Lilith in the third has strong capable hands, yet is sensitive enough to do the most delicate sculptures or extremely intricate work. The condition of the mind can many times be seen by the condition or movements of the hands, as hands are an important symbol of communication through touch or gesture. If there are psychic signatures, there may be a gift for psychometry. Where there are medical signatures, they may have healing hands. If musical, there may be the ability to conduct or they may have an unusually broad stretch on the piano.

Lilith purges the desire nature as Saturn disciplines material coping. Both create consistent awareness of where and in what we are lacking. In reference to Sepharial's affinity between these two bodies, as Saturn works to structure activities for further social maturity, Lilith works to depersonalize our desire nature for further emotional growth. Be assured that when third house matters are a problem, it is your own naive or childishly self-centered expectancies that create the problem in communication, or that bring out inferior feelings in the person associated with that house with which the individual must cope.

Lilith in the Fourth House
The emotional nature is unusually subjective; in other words, extremely personalized, insecure, and dependent on responses from others, starting with the family. These people never completely feel that they are a part of the family, feeling strangely overshadowed by them or as though they're unseen. They feel somehow denied of the emotionally satisfying activities of home life. They need to depersonalize more in order to develop some objectivity toward their exaggerated emotional dependence and their incredibly self-centered expectations.

Early in life there are frustrating emotional dead-ends where the usual family supports are concerned. In a great many instances this is because of the absence, circumstances, or temperament of the parent of the opposite sex. There may have been an illness, removal (divorce), or the actual loss of that parent, which the child may have selfishly resented with feelings of "How could he (she) do this to me!" Feeling this denial so acutely, he or she may shut out the remaining parent simply for being there, as if it were the parent's fault, not realizing this parent needs understanding and support. On the other hand, it may be that the parent of the opposite sex is totally involved in worldly things, is intellectually inclined, or otherwise impersonal. The parent may have provided well enough for the child's material necessities, but was otherwise oblivious to his or her emotional needs. In a positive chart this may in time force the child out of his or her total emotional self-involvement (because of the parent's example of impersonality), in which case the parent is capable of inspiring the child's creative interests or encouraging his or her fine mind. Or, if a negative chart, it may create a state in which the child finds it frustrating to relate to the opposite sex in later life. In the fourth Lilith may also represent a step-parent or conditions between the parents that make the home barren or uncomfortable. Many times there is a broken home. Lilith here may denote an orphan or life in a foster home.

Lilith magnifies the desires of the house it is in, and thus on the personal level in the fourth, family dependence is incredibly exaggerated. Until these people finally relate themselves to some impersonal or outside interest that will stimulate their objectivity, they can react to family with sudden petulance, hostility or defeatism without any seemingly apparent provocation. Ordinarily they can be the sweetest or the quietest of children, but may remain unusually immature into adulthood until forced, by the sheer frustration of feeling emotionally rejected, to concentrate on other areas of themselves and develop an impersonality that protects them from their naive expectations. What seems like early defiance may be the first positive step to be the individual becoming his or her own person. In its way it is a step in the right direction: to begin to independently act on his or her own decisions in order to grow up and away from his or her roots, which are impossible to emotionally satisfy (or find satisfaction in). These people have strong public attunement, and are capable of learning much from social experiences.

When negative, Lilith creates unreasoning (or neurotic) fear of rejection. Thus, in the fourth house, attitudes and reactions of others are taken far too personally. As an automatic tactical defense, there is a constant effort to please and to set (or subtly force, if necessary) the pace they can emotionally handle in relationships. The first step toward growing out of emotional dependence occurs when they substitute (not by choice at first) a creative release, mental interests, or a vocation from which to reap satisfaction, and discover a delicious sense of independence from or within family. These people are different from their family, with different needs in order to further their emotional maturity. The sooner they accept this the sooner can they objectively deal with it or the memories of youth, and put into perspective the feelings of having been misunderstood, overlooked, or cast aside.

The home is extremely important to those with Lilith in the fourth house because it is here that they must basically deal with their subjective nature. As adults, rather than live where they feel uncomfortable, which does not take much if they cannot get the cooperation they need, they prefer to live alone or withdraw from the home as much as possible. This is not meant to detract from their graciousness or kindness, but rather to protect themselves from possible emotional inroads they do not feel they can objectively deal with. Keeping away from any troubled waters is a strong consideration in their lives and a necessity for their peace of mind.

They learn to guard their emotions, yet they have a congeniality that is sincerely meant to relax others. When positive, they give the impression of going through life with the least disruption possible, but others would be wise to go along with the paramters they set. They know the pace they can handle and their sensitive antennae are always out lest they offend or be offended. When they are not ready to face a situation they simply make themselves unavailable.

Their homes are geared by their standards for the comfort of those under their roof. They may fret needlessly over trifles if they suspect discontent, giving so much reassurance to those around them as to risk the very dis-ease they fear. As hosts or hostesses they are hospitable and see to the comfort of others that belies the continuous effort behind it. There is talent here (if the rest of the chart supports it) for professional work as a hotel manager, restaurant host or hostess, or any commercial area where people meet to relax and enjoy hospitality. There may be a talent for acting because of the mood attunement they develop. Lilith aspecting an angular Moon in Cancer or Scorpio could denote talent for medicine, particularly if Lilith is in a water sign.

When Lilith is in the fourth house and marriage is the problem, investigate this area as very possibly the eroding factor between the couple. If a male, the individual is not above having set up or being drawn to another home environment where he feels more comfortable, or to one who is more conducive to providing him with what he wants. Many times this may explain why he supposedly works later and later everyday at the office.

The fourth house also represents subconscious goals, the level of which is externalized by the atmosphere of the kind of home in which one can be happy. These people can indeed be happier in a home atmosphere in which they can express an artistic flair or musical ability, enjoy a hobby, or establish a studio or office for studies or special interest, writing, student or literary gatherings. This is because Lilith is deeply satisfying and productive of positive results when motivated along objective or creatively expressive lines. As the subconscious goals (fourth house) for these people are now in need of rising to more mental, creative, or spiritual levels of unfoldment, so must the atmosphere and purpose of the home they occupy reflect this. There must be more of the yellow ray of the mind and the creative ray of the spirit allowed here for more objective fulfillment. This is needful now for the further emotional growth of these individuals.

In several cases, individuals spoke of finding satisfaction in a communal living situation because of the detachment they felt that it liberated them from emotional overdependency. They claimed to have felt a deeper family feeling among with peers because of the detachment that could more easily be maintained in an environment with no personal ties, or in one that was geared to a bohemian lifestyle, creative release, spiritual development, or service.

If one with Lilith in the fourth is an intellectual type, there is a natural detachment with family members that asserts itself as the individual matures. At best they seek to better understand family members and thus accept the differences with less resentment. However, during sentimental times such as holidays or when a family member needs emotional support, these people feel strangely removed, as if acting out a part. They will remain no longer than necessary, fearing the breakdown of their hard-won emotional self-sustainment.

The fourth house also rules the later years, when satisfaction must come from having become totally independent, mentally occupied, or creatively or otherwise productive. Nothing else will do. Lilith will be the strongest factor in the personality at this time. Ordinarily speaking, they will have developed the Lilithian impersonality about life, a love of and the wherewithal to travel, or be completely self-sustaining as a result of their lifelong turning to vocational and ocial areas. Dorothy Vanderpool, wife of Dale Carnegie, who has Lilith in the fourth house, successfully carried on her husband's business after his death in 1955. She, significantly, wrote a book entitled *Don't Grow Old, Grow Up.*

Marilyn Monroe had Lilith in the fourth house. She was brought up in foster homes and had a lonely and often cruel childhood. In her career she was exploited as a sex symbol, yet she had that strange quality of a little girl lost that stirred sympathetic feelings from her audiences. It is said that when Lilith is severely trapped it wants to die. Marilyn Monroe died of a drug overdose.

Lilith in the Fifth House
People with Lilith in the fifth house have a magnified need to express their will, their differentness, their place in the Sun—and secretly abhor being grouped. Their special need and exaggerated urge for a totally individualized expression about themselves indirectly influences their major decisions in life. Eventually they will cut themselves off from anything that threatens to obstruct this freedom. It could be dropping out of school, out of relationships, or out of parenthood unless some alternative is found so that the feeling (fear) of being put into the shadows can be tolerated for a time. No matter the chart, these people are all individualists and will sooner or later stand out in some way.

Early in life there are insecurities that spring from a haunting fear of being denied their essential difference from others—to be seen in their own light, to be unique. They feel strangely threatened when easy confidences are being exchanged by others, as if they are being somehow diminished in importance. This is not obvious, and is even sublimated for a time because Lilith is a deep, nagging need they do not always understand until suddenly, for what seems no apparent reason, they do or say something jarring that abruptly brings them special attention—good, bad or indifferent. This finally releases their built up anxiety, as if to say, "How dare you cast a shadow over my light." A case in point is of the young man who as a child loved his older brother well enough, but suddenly for no immediate reason would hit him sharply on the head when he felt overshadowed by him. Now both are grown, and although there is otherwise a strong bond of respect and affection between them, the younger one firmly maintains just enough distance to keep the other from diminishing him in importance. This example describes the why behind the occasional separativeness or deliberate personal independence these people may display from time to time with anyone close whose individualism might overshadow them. Barring this, there may be extreme insistence on being ignored, as a reverse tactic for attention through noninclusion.

In aggressive charts, particularly in youth, these people can be foolishly naive in their desire for special attention or undying affection, only to be drawn into frustrating situations. The result forces some "growing up" the hard way about affairs of the heart. When selfishly oriented, understandable in the vulnerable years of youth, and to whatever extent is the reactive temperament, ego frustration eventually surfaces as a rebellious action that seems incredibly foolish, self-defeating, unfair, or unnecessarily cruel to another, which it is. In subjective charts the individual may succeed in attracting the wrong kind of attention, until eventually, they become the recipient of such treatment—as in the case of undermining another's marriage only to have his or her own undermined.

When supported by other significators in the chart, Lilith in the fifth house may indicate a child out of wedlock, abortion, or giving away a child. There may be a long held secret here. Conversely, pregnancy itself may be denied due to a fault in the regenerative system that needs attention. Or it may be that the unconscious fear of some necessary sublimation of the ego within parenthood during the formative years of the child creates the very tension that frustrates conception. Lilith in the fifth may denote older step-children with which they may be quite happy. These people do not really care for little children because of the emotional demands it puts on them, making them feel strangely cancelled out. If the youngster is old enough to show or accept an interest that expresses his or her mind or imagination, parental rapport can begin. Otherwise, they secretly (to be sure) abhor the lack of individuality, resent the situation, or feel trapped. They may take excellent care of the essential needs but in a rather impersonal way, finding leisure time outlets to occupy them as an individual in their own right rather than as someone's parent. It is not for lack of caring as much as it is for the fact that they cannot successfully surrender themselves to the impingement on their individuality, or tolerate for too long a time denial of their desire to do as they will. As parents they can be as conscientious as any other if the rest of the chart so indicates, but they are by far more demanding in seeing to it that the youngster becomes self-sustaining at as early an age as possible. They see children more as little adults. Care for their practical needs is logical they reason, but if the truth were known they prefer them when they are older. In its highest outlet here, Lilith can be the parent who inspires talent and mental abilities in youngsters.

In a receptive, nonaggressive chart, when selfishly oriented, these people may attract sweethearts by whom they are plagued from time to time by ridiculously rebellious ploys for attention. The reason is to discover the secret of handling hysterical emotional outbursts. When they attempt to consistently handle the problem with a logical appeal, quietly but firmly showing the impracticality and humiliating aspect of their actions, they discover in themselves a confidence they never knew they were capable of. They discover the constructive use of their will that surprisingly attracts a positive response, and understand the tendency to overdramatize every action and response. They eventually discover, by pointing it out to another, that the important thing is to look at things rationally or from the viewpoint of another—in other words, impersonally. Here lies the key to unlocking Lilith's beneficial effects in the fifth. Truly, these people will discover the most gratifying expression of themselves in relationships within shared creative interests or where there is intellectual rapport. The love nature is strong, with an exaggerated sense of pleasure. So unless desire is for satisfaction within a creative, mental, or esthetic climate, the love life is indeed traumatic.

Lilith's symbol, having only the slightly slanted diagonal line cutting through the circle, represents almost no allowance for the weaknesses of the flesh, as shown by the horizontal line in the cross of matter. In connection with such overtones Lilith's effects are distinctly denying. In an air dominated or strongly Uranian chart, for instance, the impersonal element is more natural in the makeup. It more readily brings out the higher talents in the fifth house. On the contrary, in this case it might be the emotionally demanding Moon position that one needs to adjust to. For the naturally more self-centered superficial level, Lilith by house is as denying to selfish pleasure, pride, and possessiveness as Saturn is to misdirected activity-of which Lilith is as much the handmaiden, as the Moon is to the Sun. Lilith calls for detachment from the lower desires and satisfactions of its house affairs for further emotional maturing. Thus, when individuals depersonalize here (forgets about self), they find joy in avocations or creative efforts that utilize the mind and imagination.

To a certain extent, Lilith in the fifth house parallels the meaning of Lilith in Leo, as the natural ruler of both is the Sun. The difference is that in the sign the individuality and impersonal creative drive are deeply focused in the character, coloring the whole chart. But in the house Lilith represents where it is important that this be developed for further emotional growth. In a great many instances it indicates a very necessary avocational interest that these individuals need in order to round out the ego—to grow up and out of themselves emotionally. Otherwise, ego problems create much unhappiness. More than to simply protect exaggerated willfulness, they need to depersonalize in their affections. Rather than through emotionalism, where they are not above narcissim, they need to shine through talents of the mind or imagination, where wells of lower energy are translated into riches of the spirit.

Lilith's urges are compelling, make no mistake about that, and are the basis of psychological fears related to this house. Creativity is what is chafing for release into the conscious mind, once emotional static is cleared—or as a way to clear it. Invariably, when these people relate to higher desires of the mind rather than emotion, they find an alternative route for pleasureable adventure through an artistic, technical, or mentally challenging expression of strong will. This includes any of the various arts or crafts or through a specific area of the vocation which they can give their own individual coloring, specialty, or style. More often than not these people appear to be mostly self-taught in their specialty. Whether it is recognized, even appreciated, is not as important to them as the self-confidence and personal satisfaction they find in its creative release. These people are capable of spiraling an avocation into an important part of what they do.

However, if these people cannot depersonalize enough, they have a dogmatic and rather dictatorial manner, no matter the effort to justify it in argument or to couch it in polite remarks; they also can be deliberate omissions in conversation. The constant fear of becoming lost in the crowd underlies a near panic that creates an overbearing manner. It can be the extremes of arrogance or the over-dramatization of activity simply to capture attention (as in extroverted types) or the extreme of non-commitment that leaves others waiting for the other shoe to drop (as in introverted types). In this case there can be a deliberately exaggerated emphasis on pulling back in activities for some reason, becoming so inobvious as to be obvious by their absence or constant retreats. Either way, the ego desire to attract attention is served. In all cases, though, these people may deny it, or go to great lengths to appear just the opposite. There is a take-charge attitude that is surprisingly efficient when it is dedicated to the success of a project as opposed to personal gratification (theirs or anyone else's). It is successful in the case of the rearing of children for their mental/creative/spiritual development as opposed to concentration on the satisfaction of emotional-material wants.

They can be excellent though not necessarily orthodox teachers. When work is the primary issue, there is the ability to inspire talent or confidence in another through enthusiastic belief in their ability so as to actually fascinate the person into more deeply believing in himself or herself. No greater love can a person demonstrate than this. This in turn reflects a warmth of appreciation back to them, the satisfaction of which is found to be far greater than any other they could otherwise receive.

There is a strong desire for the spotlight and the drama, which accounts for many of these people being attracted to the field of entertainment or politics. Among dictators is Adolf Hitler. Among writers is O. Henry, who dramatically individualized even the most ordinary of people.

Lilith in the Sixth House
These people are at their best when working under conditions that allow plenty of room for independence, imagination, ingenuity, and decisiveness. They are among the most resourceful and conscientious workers, and have an amazing eye for detail that challenges the mind or makes use of a strong imagination. When positive, they can successfully maintain a thoroughly helpful, but nonetheless impersonal, relationship with those who share their working environment. They prefer to leave emotional types, personal matters, and opinions totally aside while on the job because of the impossible distractions it creates for them personally. They feel strangely trapped otherwise, threatened or overshadowed when personalities, bringing emotional overtones rather than work abstraction, dominate the environment. They can be any type of personality otherwise, depending on the chart, but while working are more inspired (inspiring) and gratified when they are mentally or creatively preoccupied to the exclusion of all else. They take the independence and prerogatives they need in order to maintain their sensitivity to what they are doing rather than to the surrounding environment.

Under ordinary working conditions, where simple routines are repeatedly carried out allowing for little or no outlet of the creative intellect or imagination, people with Lilith in the sixth house get absolutely no satisfaction. In fact, quite the opposite is true. They feel frustrated and are apt to develop strong resentment, which eventually is undermining to their health or creates work related problems due to negative or defeatist attitudes. When negative these people are usually introverted or emotionally-oriented types concerning work, who consciously or not have a subjective attitude on the job. This is as opposed to the impersonal, professional, or executive attitude Lilith is trying to push into their consciousness. They feel trapped in endless routine and grow restless unless they have some independent or executive capacity that allows them the freedom to use their time as they will so long as the job is done and it challenges them.

Lilith creates incredible sensitivity to precision, detail, executive usefulness, and an exaggerated conscientiousness that is out of proportion for simple or routine work—that is, unless some outlet is found where the mental juices or their inventive imagination can flow. There is otherwise too much time for personal preoccupation. The unreleased imagination on their more productive mental level then turns the strong critical powers inward to give rise to illness, imagined slights from coworkers, and in some cases an unreasonable preoccupation with health that borders on or reaches hypochondria.

In the sixth house Lilith creates tension concerning technicalities because of the magnification of the perfectionistic drive. Unless these people work in a position where there is sufficient outlet for the mental precision and remarkable creative ingenuity, they find it impossible to become sufficiently detached in order to rise above the personal (or petty things). They feel oddly out of place, inferior, fearful, or resentful, depending upon the chart. The specific need and deep desire for independence, a mental/creative outlet, or an executive or specialized capacity is a prime necessity in their work world. They are natural executives, given the chance. Otherwise, these people can become the hermits, troublemakers, sirens, or the Don Juans of the office, with something distinctly uncomfortable about their personalities.

The magnified work consciousness, when unsatisfied, seeds a nagging sense of uselessness they feel or a carefully guarded resentment. They sense that an important innovative part of themselves is missing in what they do. It accounts for sudden irrational behavior, rudeness, coldness, or in the more timid types it may take the form of a health upset. They may be unreasonably sensitive or so strongly distant that others around them cannot escape being affected.

When negative, job insecurity is exaggerated no matter the position held. They secretly fear being replaced by those around them because egosim, negative attitudes or work simply for routine gain magnifies a feeling of being expendable. They will not trust or confide in anyone. It is the factor of detachment that makes the difference. There can be many job changes until these people learn to depersonalize, in which case they ambitiously seek or begin working toward a position they know they're qualified for. Then they will gravitate quite naturally to work that takes advantage of this precision and management or creative talents. Lilith is extreme, either way.

There is talent for unusual services, depending upon the chart, for work in the psychic fields, parapsychology, or any offbeat occupation. They thrive on the challenge and do not particularly care about its acceptability if they feel it has useful substance or satisfies an appetite for the bizarre.

When early work attitudes are superficial, individuals can, for example, be happy and successful in their college work but put off graduation one way or the other in order to stay in the mental climate. They would rather not face the prospect of routine work even though it is an unconscious decision. There are those among them who may find themselves attracting easy romantic involvements on the job because Lilith creates a disarming magnetism in the house it occupies. This may temporarily serve to assert their difference from co-workers, or they may gain identity through others who are doing what they would like to do. It overcomes a sickening sense of facelessness for a time, but it will only end up in further frustration. Office romances, or those with someone who shares their job interest and whose work they admire, can easily fall into this category. These people are foolish if they think it can be anything more. The problem is within themselves, not outside. It stems primarily from a naive attitude that this will solve their frustration instead of accepting that they must express through their own work rather than reflecting that of others.

In positive charts these people are highly intelligent, usually executive workers capable of the kind of detachment that makes for excellent critical powers and efficiency. Most of them, and more so the extroverted types—Virgo Suns, planets in Virgo, or those having the Sun prominent—discover very early that when personalities are allowed to enter into work, their perspective is lost. This would bring out a negative or complaining nature, theirs or someone else's, and there would be concentration on negative things that are self-defeating in the end. In this case they find themselves subjected to complaints from others who selfishly take up their time with problems for which they do not want a solution as much as they want a sympathetic ear.

For employers with Lilith in the sixth house it is wise to remember that employees are at their best in their jobs when personal resourcefulness is stimulated and allows for the independent spirit.

In a male chart, female employees are career-oriented and ambitious. Never underestimate this. They can become undermining and quite negative if they are subjected to a secondary role because of gender, either in actuality or by attitude. Recognize this, or you will probably wish you had.

Lilith in the Seventh House
The partner has an unusually strong personality due to deep identity needs and is usually career-oriented, intelligent, and quite talented in his or her own right. However, in personal life the partner cannot successfully identify with the native's emotional give and take. He or she feels strangely alien to it, intimidated, or overshadowed, contrary to outer appearances, giving rise to sudden outbreaks of resentful behavior. Unfaithfulness is not uncommon; of course this is not always necessarily the case, depending on other stabilizing factors in the chart. Nevertheless, the suspicion of it is experienced by the chart owner, probably due to the dependent-independ-

ent enigma that is the mate. This is what creates a serious problem of emotional incompatibility between them. If the native married in order to gain an emotional security blanket, then the marriage is based on a naive premise. It is here that Lilith's (emotionally maturing) denials will force the individual to outgrow his or her emotional expectancies via the perspective gained by having to deal with this in a mate. Marital difficulties are directly connected to the partner's inability to detach from emotionally selfish expectations in relationships that unwittingly create a deteriorating competitiveness between the two, and the chart owner's failure to see it. Feeling abandoned, the mate abandons. Feeling denied, the mate denies.

The partner deeply and primarily needs vocational interests or a strong social-creative expression of the self. The partner needs such impersonal activity in order to depersonalize enough from the self to release unique talent, and through this enjoy the personal fulfillment he or she feels denied of otherwise. This mate needs the detachment from personal preoccupation with self that intellectual, creative, or vocational activities demand in order to bring out an unusually fine mind, creative flair, or enjoyable work. This is where the mate's self-confidence, self-respect, and personal satisfaction must come from in order to finally feel the self-image that Lilith flatly denies in the private, more emotionally oriented, partnership life. Any outlets such as the literary or artistic fields, public works, or job involvement where one can use the initiative are the real growth needs. This is as opposed to being subjected to the emotional needs and personality of the chart owner, home or family, where he or she can be incredibly naive or childish in expectancies due to serious lack of self-perspective and continual need for assurance of devotion.

In the seventh, Lilith literally magnifies the need for the chart owner to accept the sunset of his or her personal selfish desires in relationships for the greater development of impersonal interactivity between self and another. Lilith in the seventh house magnifies the classic Libra principle of emotional detachment in order to balance a situation. Anything less blinds one's perspective in dealing responsibly in relationships and particularly in marriage.

Lilith denies the usual partnership satisfactions on personal-emotional levels unless at this level the marriage serves a mutual purpose that is above the strictly personal ego considerations for either one. In this case the completion of the purpose brings to an apparent end the mutual gratification or the need to remain together. However, it is one which no doubt serves to bring the native a long way toward emotional maturity from false expectations in relationships, or at least to some self-objectivity in relationships for having had the experience. This is exactly what Lilith in the social seventh house are all about.

In several case histories the purpose of the couple's remaining together was the rearing of the children, regardless of their own desires. In another, because of deep mutual concern, the couple was cooperatively working together to help create a special care center for their handicapped child. Within the impersonality of concern for something above themselves, they discovered their own particular kind of working relationship. In still another, the native's need was to deliberately steer the wife toward establishing herself in a career or profession. This was the only way he could extricate himself from the suffocation he felt as a result of her total emotional dependence on him at one time, and then resentment of being dependent on him at another. Her dependence stemmed from an overblown inferiority complex and emotional immaturity, creating naive and surprisingly childish expectations from this otherwise independent and intelligent person. It is a curious enigma. The native spoke of feeling that the end of the relationship was at hand when a purpose he had served for the creative growth of the partner had ended. He agreed that within its fulfillment a great deal of his own "growing-up" had taken place. Suffice it to say that as impersonally demanding as Saturn is within material duties, so in a like manner is Lilith impersonal and demanding of objectivity within relationships. Anything less continues the native's emotional frustration in marriage and problems in key relationships. This may sound cold, even impossible, but Lilith matures, regardless of sentiment.

If the union is originally based on shared vocational, intellectual, or creative interests mutually enjoyed, the two can be of great inspiration, help, or a source of pride to one another. But at no time can the native successfully limit the partner to just the personal life, even if that is what the partner may think he or she wants. This invites an eventual breakdown of communication. Within such an atmosphere the individual is constantly subjected to the subtle, unpredictable, and often incredible demands of an emotionally insecure partner. Lilith liberates, and in the seventh house is representative of a partner who must live in an equally independent atmosphere or become cold and draining.

Separative problems arise when the native loses (or never had) the personal objectivity to see where the frustration was coming from or, mutually, they have done something together that is now finished, ending their "we are" cycle of action. The resulting void allows for personal ego expressions of the native to naturally emerge that threaten to shut out the partner's constantly magnified need for expression equal to his, unwittingly denying the partner his or her place. For any other couple the adjustment might occur simply by the partner stepping aside or playing a lesser role. Not so for one with a seventh house Lilith. When the mate loses his or her sense of equality in the native's life, to the native's new and seemingly superior interest without sufficient vocational or creative releases of his or her own, the vacuum is quickly filled with secret fears of denial, deep resentment and/or impossible demands. This is draining on the chart owner, and it leaves the mate no happier for it. We need to remember that Lilith encourages success in relationships on impersonal levels (vocational, creative, artistic, intellectual, or true friendship), but discourages them on the petty or emotional levels, because pure and simply it has no reality here. For the chart owner to support, indeed to push, the mate's talent efforts or vocational growth is to help the mate become liberated from the dependence that the Lilithian nature inwardly abhors, and from which there is mutual benefit.

The partner has great loyalty and pride in the chart owner's accomplishments, as this is the impersonal area where they relate best. However, there are apparently no great feelings of disloyalty should he or she stray because Lilith creates feelings in the partner of being unfairly trapped and unappreciated in emotional interactions. There is no doubt that the chart owner will grow, one way or the other, to the objectivity he or she critically needs when Lilith is in the seventh house. Usually the chart owner has a strong ego which the partner sensed and admired at the outset of the attraction, but also because of which the feeling of competition later arises in the marriage. It appears that the native looked upon marriage as a convenience, and was attracted to one who, although intelligent and talented, only appeared to be independent and emotionally strong. In reality, the individual was too emotionally immature for a serious personal relationship.

From this we can relate to the large number of problems reported for a seventh house Lilith, considering the hopefully passing norm for one partner to be the dominant one. Lilith's impersonal emphasis in relationships does not allow for dominance or control in marriage (eighth house psychology), parental substitute roles (fourth-tenth psychology); a servant mentality (sixth), or security for the other (second). It magnifies equality and mutually respected independence found only in the clean impersonality of a sincere friendship, which is the foundation for needed objectivity during times of emotional crisis, the burden of which falls to the native because Lilith is in his or her relationship house. The equally strong self-projective partner who needs or appreciates encouragement for his or her talents, reacts with a truly fascinating and cooperative personality in this case. It is only the blindspot in the partner's emotional ego that gives form to all manner of discontent, deceit, or hysteria. Be realistic about the partner's rather liberated views concerning marriage; because the problem occurs when either one denies it. Lilith is truly an Aquarian Age symbol when in the seventh house. Likened to Uranus in the seventh, which signifies a relationships based on friendship or intellectual ties, Lilith in this house can create a comfortable atmosphere for living together. Marriage for one with Lilith in the seventh is best for one who is successful in his or her own right, and primarily a loyal friend, as opposed to the emphasis on emotional security and sexual love as the basis of the union. It is possible.

Lilith entering the area above the horizon indicates that it is the acceptance of the self as part of a unit, as opposed to selfish preoccupation, that is being worked out in the native. Probably it is some of both, as none of us is totally objective or subjective. After all, the seventh house shows how the world reacts to our projections. The partner as the Not Self mirrors the chart owner's own level of social maturity (or immaturity), accounting for the original attraction. The process of living with it then becomes a lesson in perspective. To run away from problems before reasonable attempts are made to work them out is to run away from a part of yourself within a growth experience that will only repeat itself in another relationship. If you accept the affinity Sepharial spoke of between Lilith and Saturn, you will better understand the commanding atmosphere for achievement and detachment from ego that they both force in the house they each motivate.

Lilith in the Eighth House

Loner tendencies are strong in these people, but are deliberately kept to a low profile. This is to insure that attention is not drawn to their uncommonly deep need for privacy, and create the kind of curiosity about themselves that invites questions, leaving them vulnerable to intrusions or influences over which they have no control. They have a strong aversion for idle curiosity and expediently conduct themselves in a manner so as not to arouse it. These people need a certain amount of solitude in order to first develop and then maintain a greatly needed objectivity in a world toward which their reactions are intense in one way or another. Lilith is extreme, no middle ground. In the eighth house it magnifies the introverted tendencies in the individual and particularly the desire nature, creating an intense inner life. In solitude they find the strengthening peace they need. No matter the tone of the chart otherwise, privacy is a fetish.

Though the appearance may be one of being direct and outwardly involved (extroverted), they are nevertheless discreet in building a private life for themselves that makes them not easily accessible, either through choice of residence, lifestyle, or work immersion. Living a good distance from relatives and friends, or having to work odd hours, offers an acceptable and non-neglectful reason for not visiting, thereby insuring greater solitude for themselves. They care as deeply, if not more than others, for their loved ones and friends, but must be infinitely more particular of the inroads even those with the best of intentions can make. No matter how it is done, it allows for the privacy they want—even a desire for anonymity—without drawing undue notice that might attract interference, misinterpretation, or denial of self-control in their own lives. They are secretive about being secretive.

The unusually strong need for privacy, sensed in childhood, is eventually hidden in the makeup. This is partly to deny something in themselves they are unsure they can handle and partly to conform to the group in order to insure acceptance—no small consideration in childhood and youth. It nevertheless results in few, but very special friends. Keeping their own counsel becomes quite automatic in adulthood. They take great care not to give any unnecessary indications of their thoughts, opinions, or plans until they have had enough time alone to thoroughly investigate and formulate them and to make certain that they are in control of any plan and themselves. They do not want to risk being undermined or attract unnecessary opposition.

They feel strangely vulnerable, and are, which explains the early tensions or resentment. As they grow older, they are continually haunted by uneasy feelings of losing all control of their affairs to others, or of being victimized. This may be entirely subconscious, but accounts for another of the unusual psychological fears that many astrologers have found in the house Lilith tenants. They learn sooner or later that naive behavior brings just that, and that premature discussion dissipates the thrust of what they want to do. After all, this is the house of social standards and moral values other than their own, the house where outside values have the greater power of intimidation to compromise them and subject them to the control of others or existing opinion. They must build their psychic-emotional defenses through the objectivity they gain from an intellectual or strictly practical approach to things, or through a creative ambition that supplies an impersonal social outlet through which their intensity can be productively channeled, or enslaved to circumstances with no options. This is not to imply any lack of personal sincerity or graciousness on their part (unless other factors indicate otherwise), but simply a far greater than average need to get for themselves the necessary time and the necessary space for objectivity with which to insure their privacy. Anything less becomes secretly abhorrent to them. Indeed, it is crucial for their further emotional development, or they learn the hard way that untested trust (naivete) keeps them in a compromising position. Contrary to outer appearances of congeniality, these are very private people with extremely fixed feelings.

When these people are unselfishly or impersonally oriented, Lilith in the eighth house releases solid inner guidance for raising consciousness through challenges of the mind, the imagination, or the spirit, as opposed to mundane desire. When they do finally raise the consciousness above mere superficial satisfactions (or are forced to) and accept that their path is through something higher in themselves, they gain and keep control of their lives and are at peace. No amount of invested wealth, marital or social support, inheritance, or even power can achieve the same satisfaction. When selfishly oriented, they keep reaching for more because they are their powerful desire nature denies the higher Lilithian energy; this only results in frustration. Until they relate to the riches of the mind, the soul, or the spirit, as opposed to the weaknesses of the flesh and the desires of the personality, they can never feel totally satisfied. This is realized earlier in life in those who have a chart that is intellectual, creative, or strongly Uranian because it indicates natural objectivity.

When positive, they often find satisfying release through a vocational pursuit that has within it an outlet, no matter how direct or indirect, for a particular talent of the sign Lilith is in. It gives their work the sign's special coloring and it makes it unique from others in their field. Vocational pursuit is satisfying, and because of its impersonality it finally frees them from the grip of social insecurity by giving them a more secure social identity. Eventually, there is an acquired strength that one can sense about these people, and that makes some uneasy. Although they will forgive a slight, they will never forget it. Pride is strong. They are turned off by mediocrity, but have near reverence for high achievers, excellence, and perseverance.

The eighth is the house of sexual orientation, so it is not unusual to find instances of homosexuality in people with this placement. In one instance the husband was a transexual and in another, an extremely negative case, the father was incestuous. When negative, people with Lilith in the eighth house may be subject to perverse sexuality from a mate, or at the other end of the spectrum, rejection, either of which are rooted in inhibitions in the partner that stem from serious emotional insecurity (immaturity).

Usually at least once in youth these people are in a position where they have no control (possibly because of foolishly entering into a situation where base desires dominated), finding themselves compromised, controlled, severely criticized, or totally misunderstood. They felt the sickening feeling of humiliation and the stinging loss of pride. Through such an experience or through one that came close too close for comfort, particularly in a passive chart, they realize how vulnerable they are. They also realize the critical need for at least partially distancing themselves from others in order to develop objectivity by becoming more observant.

In some cases it is through the early death of someone very close, witnessing a near death or fatal accident, or through work that brings them into contact with death and brings an awareness of the fragility of life. This is magnified by Lilith and creates a metaphysical awareness of their own mortality—the open sesame to objectivity.

The eighth is also the house of healing and powers of regeneration. Some form of healing may be another area of interest to people with an eighth house Lilith. Lilith focuses awareness of this ability through which healing is channeled, and each time healing is practiced it also results in self-healing.

They are proud, which when positive translates into ambition and dedicated work. There is a personal dignity that is quietly but consistently impressive. This was deeply admired in theater star Helen Hayes and film star Spencer Tracy. Tracy's memorable performance in Hemingway's *The Old Man and the Sea* aptly describes the solitude and the incredible spartan perseverance Lilith in the eighth makes one capable of identifying with on its higher level.

There is nowhere on Earth that offers greater solitude than the North and South Poles, which Admiral Richard E. Byrd felt challenged to explore and conquer. He was the first man to fly over these areas, and he successfully headed expeditions into the forbidding Antarctic regions, establishing a base there called Little America on the Ross Ice Shelf at the Bay of Whales (see chart 8). Lilith, co-ruler of the Ascendant in Virgo in the eighth house, clearly describes Admiral Byrd's personal exhiliration and tremendous fascination for the strangeness, ruggedness, and supreme solitude of the untouched worlds he felt driven to explore and chart. Lilith's position in Virgo in the eighth combined to bring out a spartanism in him that aided him in withstanding the physical rigors of those lonely and treacherous journeys. Lililth sextile Mercury, ruler of the ninth, and Uranus tenanting this house, explains his consuming interest and determination to explore the most remote corners of Earth, as if searching for some kind of truth breakthrough for himself by overcoming so forbidding a region.

The literary explorations of Marc Edmund Jones, Manly Palmer Hall, and C.E.O. Carter took them into the finer world of the occult. Carter, particularly in his book *The Zodiac and the Soul*, reveals the great sensitivity and preoccupation Lilith magnifies in this house as "the doorway to the world beyond." In one way or another these are impressive people. There is something of the explorer-investigator in them when manifesting positively, whether it be of the geography, the mind, or the soul. These people can become legendary figures in their fields because of their consistently excellent performance in their work and the absence of the small personality from view, lending a mystique that puts them a cut above the ordinary.

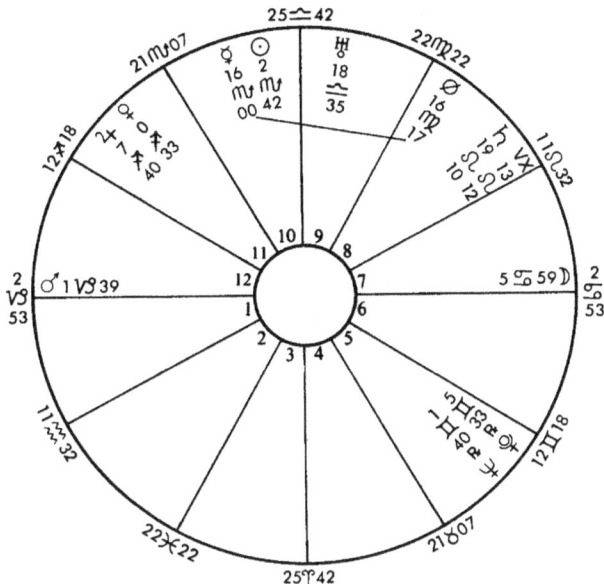

Chart 8. Admiral Richard E. Byrd, October 25, 1888, 11:30 a.m., Winchester, Virginia; source: Mother

There is something of the arch reformer in them, as observed in singer Anita Bryant's unrelenting nationwide effort in the 1970s to prevent homosexuality from receiving open acceptance. Her convictions regarding sexuality were obviously magnified into a crusading psychology. With Lilith in the Scorpio decanate of Pisces opposition Neptune retrograde and sextile a tenth house Mars-Uranus-Venus conjunction, she claimed to have been "called to the cause" and would not stop until she saw it through. Her conviction to then work to "have these souls reborn to Christ" is significant of the level of commitment typical of these people, right or wrong.

There can be activity in bringing about gender equality and societal reforms, ranging from Helen Gurley Brown's *Sex and the Single Girl* (Lilith in Libra square Pluto retrograde) to black feminine activist Angela Davis (Lilith at 1 Capricorn square Neptune), who spoke out on the decadence of American contemporary society; to Martin Luther King, who crusaded for civil rights, to the many others with the position of Lilith in the natal or solar eighth who were active in or sympathetic to societal movements they believed would bring about social reforms. Whatever the direction, there appears to be an attunement to mass psychology.

Lilith in the Ninth House
Religious beliefs are unusual, unorthodox, or nonexistent. You might say these are the intellectual vagabonds of the zodiac. They are the ones who are different from the rest of the family in their philosophy, overall view of life, and lifestyle. They chafe at being locked into beliefs, dogma, set social ideas, a philosophy for living, or a lifestyle that is not their own. They must

eventually form their own interpretations in order to resolve the threat they feel from the strong sense of limitation of set ideas. They feel as if they are cancelled out by something that others accept as an abstraction, but which to them seems foreign. There is no sense of freedom of self in it. Quite the opposite. However, so long as they are not stopped in important things they want to do, this feeling is not at first obvious. If the lifestyle expected of them interferes with their desires or direction, however, it becomes a noticeable sore point.

In youth, rather than risk unnecessary attention that would expose their social differences and chance what they instinctively sense to be a threat to their most important freedom, they may go along for a time, saying nothing. This is because at this point they may not know what is missing, just that something is missing. The nonconformist ideas are particularly played down in the more timid or conservative types, lest it attract argument, criticism, opposition, or outright denial they are unsure they can handle—or, for that matter, yet understand in themselves. Nevertheless, their dress, sympathies, and lifestyle ideas eventually expose their different approach, many times creating antagonism from those who take it as a rejection. From the more direct types, it is taken as a form of rebellion or a deliberate irritant.

Only truth through knowledge can free them from the lack of intellectual identity they fear, and its accompanying inferiority complex as a result of set ideas for living and thinking that leave no room for their own philosophic expression. Until they are finally aware that this is in fact what they are looking for, they can be secretly antagonistic and appear strangely contrary or distant. You may find agnostics in this group until a way of thinking is found through which to look at life and religious concepts through the occult, the mystical, or as a result of a creative expression. They may seek truth through intellectual abstractions such as astrology, philosophy, investigation of comparative or Eastern religions, or through speculative inquiry concerning the source and nature of human knowledge.

They find it impossible to relate for long to materialistic philosophies, or traditional ideas or beliefs they may have been exposed to as children. They feel no satisfaction, outer appearances to the contrary. Things, reasons, habits, or social patterns that influenced the family directly or indirectly, and that resulted in lifestyle choices, escape them entirely. They cannot accept ideas of right or wrong, or have faith in a religious pattern for living, simply because it may be their background. Quite the contrary, it is meaningless to them, resulting in unclear ethics. They feel locked into something that is strangely stifling, and they are nagged by a haunting fear until they understand and know why. It accounts for their attitudes, which are different from the rest of the family and that may appear as odd ego trips, but which are, in fact, the release of a compulsion for free thinking that has been building up inside of them for a long time. To others their way can appear totally naive, incredibly far-out, or self-defeating, which it may very well be. Nevertheless, they need to intellectually reach out for themselves, or they will attract experiences that will one day force them to do that.

They need to test themselves, or be tested against ideas, in order to promote further emotional maturation through objective thought. Without it they will never find satisfying relief from a deep personal sense of ignorance, no matter the amount of education or mundanely satisfying lifestyle. Simply put, they must find their own truth or they are repressed in their social growth via a compatible marriage, relationships, and so on. The open sesame to Lilith's great need to *understand* in the ninth house is through questioning, searching out ideas, analyzing, and wondering, even if they must travel far or through the world of ideas as lifelong students. Once these special people impersonally search for higher answers, they begin to free themselves of the false (to them) perceptions that made them feel intellectually blocked. It is not easy, but then growth never is.

The early personalization of parental ideas exaggerates an inner sense of having no choices. It eventually attracts situations (then and/or later) that expose their fear of intellectual dependence that feeds a desperation to run. In some cases they may be forced to search for higher answers because of a partner's problems that stem from such feelings. In this case, the nagging fear is blind at first in the sense that they do not know what they feel the lack of, only that they must reach out for something more than they know in order to solve their problem. This accounts for a seeming instability to those close to them. They know something is missing but do not understand what until they finally start asking questions, even if at first only to themselves or about themselves.

On its highest level, Lilith in the ninth house is a sure guide to truth. In the ninth, Lilith creates an inquiring mind that compels a nagging itch for opposing thought, which they will then question. They will investigate the extraordinary, or even the bizarre in thought, if only to know what is there. They can raise questions that seem unanswerable to those who are content to simply (as they see it) live by traditional or social patterns even when it is self-defeating. They are considered, if not heretics, then at least irritants to those who do not care to question but accept a code, philosophy, or way of life they have never analyzed above the obvious or questioned beyond the rules laid down for reaching conclusions. Nevertheless, they stir others to thought, even if antagonistically at first. However, they prefer not to be too obvious about it lest their compelling need to understand things is seriously interfered with or denied to them. If they even suspect this coming they are apt to feign agreement, to get away from the subject, or simply leave. This is not meant to be dishonest. It is merely a protective measure against unnecessary opposition or attracting a denial through exposure of their compulsive desire to speculate, particularly if they see personalities entering into it. This stirs an emotional defensiveness in them that cancels their perspective, making them feel trapped and becoming either overbearing or sounding foolish.

They can be the most gracious of people and not at all insincere about listening to other people's ideas because of their magnified curiosity, even appearing to accept them. They learn, or will learn, the importance of putting the other person's mind to rest so that the abstraction is not lost to emotional defensiveness. At this point they would feel surprisingly inferior to the situation—and are. Ordinarily they will go to great lengths to make others feel intellectually comfortable so that they can be intellectually comfortable with them.

Jupiter rules the objective consciousness in the ninth house. It is magnified by the impersonality of Lilith, which frustrates mundane explanation. In this case Lilith would be denied, finding these people quietly amazed (and sometimes maybe a little envious) by the comfort others can take from what seems to them simplistic answers to so vast a concept as God or universality. Until they begin searching for or acting on their own objective ideas, they cannot shake a certain haunting loneliness from truth, God, and love (if they will admit it), and an irritating sense of emotional dependence they secretly abhor. Eventually these people are accepted as having the strange ideas in the family.

Many with this position gravitate to astrology, not to mention the unorthodox religions or philosophies, the paranormal, and so on in order to find their answers to questions that just will not go away. In other words, they need to objectify things for themselves and develop the vision that strengthens through knowledge or a rational idea of God. But curiously enough, all this occurs while at the same time crediting either the merits of scientific evaluation or some other traditional systematic analysis so that they appear as enigmas—neither fish nor fowl. In truth it is the better part of valor against disharmony. The scientists among them are apt to take that one step further into the unknown that threatens their credibility to the scientific community. However, their expertise at rationalization eventually stands them in good stead.

There is near reverence for knowledge, knowledgeable people, books, authors, publishers or publishing, specialized libraries, and travel. Information compulsively attracts, but not in the same sense as Gemini, which wants data; rather, it is in the sense of Sagittarius, which dwells in the larger concept of the whole no matter how far out it seems. When impersonally motivated—in other words, intellectually, creatively, or for esthetic reasons or content—these people can be unusually fine writers if other factors in the chart support it. But they are apt to water down extraordinary views in order to keep the intellectual atmosphere free of unnecessary opposition.

When unselfishly oriented, they are supportive and inspiring to those who would teach or write. They have an unusually keen eye for provocative information. When creatively oriented, they are not without superior imagination; they are the courageous forerunners of the abstract in art and thought and can be the catalysts for the broader disbursement of higher or occult knowledge for those who would seek it. They know that truth in any form does not make this universe a more difficult place to live in, but in fact makes it infinitely easier if people are clear in their understanding of it. People with Lilith in the ninth are often found in publishing, or as scouts for new material. As artists or photographers, they provoke thought by way of symbols in their choice of picturing. They may also be found in production work of foreign films or films that provoke thought through the bizarre or unusual. Among the latter is Italian film maker Federico Fellini, whose ninth house Lilith is trine his Capricorn Sun-Moon-Mercury in the fifth house to magnify supportively his creative efforts. It is also square Uranus dignified in Aquarius, stamping the bizarre, erotic, or extraordinary in the story line (see chart 9).

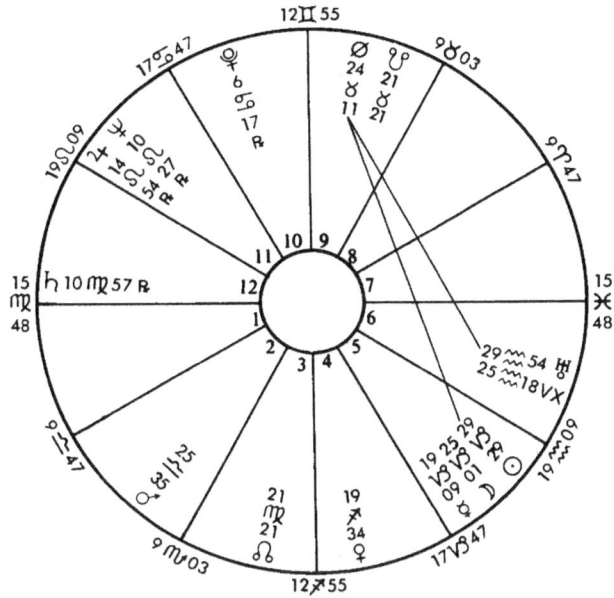

Chart 9. Federico Fellini, January 20, 1920, 9:00 p.m., Rimini, Italy; source: Penfield

Others with Lilith in the ninth house are Edgar Cayce, who created some of the most provocative published material on the popular market; and Albert Schweitzer, who did not preach philosophy as much as he lived his own. Writers are Grace Metalius, Dal Lee, and Robert Ripley; and publishers are Paul G. Clancy of *American Astrology* magazine and Robert Carl Jansky of Astro Analytics Publications.

Lilith in the Tenth House

In the tenth house, Lilith is harmoniously supportive to a career in one of the literary fields, the arts, inspirational work (the ministry or related work), and the occult. Lilith is supportive in a profession where these individuals can express the influence through the intellect, creative imagination, or in healing. It has been found that many with a tenth house Lilith have strong psychic or mediumistic leanings, because when Lilith is elevated and angular it spreads the mantle of the unusual or the "different" over the chart.

The mundane or noncreative element has no place in the worklife of those with Lilith in the tenth. This position needs a vocational release that is somehow meaningful for more than simply material or superficial gratification. Nothing else will do. There are frustrating denials, or at best, a continually nagging fear of never having a secure enough position or finding a desirable and lasting vocation. Within the ordinary, or when materialistically motivated, these people feel as though the vocational position is strangely threatened or that it's never quite enough. They feel inferior in this sector, which indeed they are. Even a position such as the presidency of a corporation could generate this feeling, as though the individual is not doing enough, and indeed he or she is not. Lilith denies and frustrates, preventing a more meaningful outlet.

The governing urge is strong, although they may deny it even to themselves. When selfishly motivated, justifiably or not, there are hidden feelings of career inadequacy, as if they are always in the wrong place. It sets up a tension others notice. Overpersonalization of themselves in the workplace stifles recognition despite good effort and results because superiors feel the individual is crowding their authority. This creates in superiors a subtle feeling or threat of being undermined by the individual at some point in the future. This is not the intention, but when they do not have creative outlet, this is the distinct impression they give, and accounts for many problems with employers. Whether or not they have this in mind, of course, depends on other factors in the chart. Nevertheless, the impression sets up an uncomfortable climate of distrust that is impossible to shake. These people sense the wall of distrust or the growing hostility of superiors, which leaves them always wanting and needing proof of job security, acceptance, and recognition. It is a vicious circle, and one which is liable to erupt in incredible personality clashes, forcing these people to settle for second best or be miserable in their work.

Public or career orientation is strong, appearances to the contrary. Family duties are taken care of insofar as necessary, but those with Lilith in the tenth house will use any excuse to get back to work. Even though the administrative talents may be superior, when personalities enter into it these people can suddenly project what strikes others as incredible immaturity through becoming blinded to the situation as a result of allowing themselves to become to personally involved. This leaves the question open as to their competence. Until, or unless, they can successfully depersonalize in the professional life—in other words, take an impersonal, intellectual, or strictly creative approach, which they critically need and what Lilith is all about in the tenth house—they cannot get nor give concrete satisfaction. Their own personality insecurity with superiors creates or attracts an impossibly strained atmosphere under which to work.

In a receptive chart (water sign rising, Moon high in the chart, Neptune in the first, many feminine planets), Lilith may manifest in the tenth house as a superior who is easily intimidated and portrays the above mentioned insecurities. From such problems these people are eventually forced into the cool impersonality they need to deal with the influence. If this is the case, the attraction stems directly from the native's own inability to develop or maintain a professional (nonpersonal) attitude. They must learn to keep these relationships strictly removed from the personality level in order to function and to keep their superiors from reacting to negative feelings of being crowded out in their authority.

Lilith's frustrations are for positive effect, to move one into work that is better suited to the talents and greater growth. Negative Lilith energy moves these people out of what they are doing and onto a level they are much better working through, comfortable or not. It must be something through which they can use their fine intellect concerning tenth house matters, powers to inspire, uncommon ideas, or creative expression in public life. Lilith's denials operate only along lines that are outgrown, indicating that impersonalization is essential before the greater talents they most certainly have can come forward. Many times this is through an unbelievably problem-filled first career or job. Suffice it to say that as impersonally demanding as Saturn is for material objectivity, so in like manner is Lilith impersonal and demanding of emotional objectivity. In this instance it is within vocational matters and professional relationships. Lilith is indifferent and matures regardless of sentiment. Otherwise it destroys, distorts, or frustrates.

Much has been written about Lilith's denying action, enough to substantiate a definite force operating at this point. However, it is logical that if Lilith works in some charts, it must work in all—with positive effects also, as not all charts are found to have difficulty here. Quite the opposite. For example in an intellectual or creative chart where the impersonal factor is a natural part of the makeup (Aquarius rising, prominent Uranus, or many air planets), problems are more easily handled or are minimal, if at all. When goals are intended in vocation for something with more meaning than simply making a living or a prestigious self-serving mark in the world, something where the higher self can express, as through writing, the arts, social-service fields, entertainment, or invention, Lilith represents a dynamic success syndrome that brings the individual incredible satisfaction. The impersonality of Lilith in the tenth inspires those who think in terms of a creative or social contribution in what they do. They may be teachers, writers, actors, school or stage directors, ministers, astrologers, or sponsors of creative expression in others. It can take in the psychic, occult or parapsychology, as these are expressed from the sensitivity level rather than the personal. Be assured these people have something meaningful to give, as Lilith is particularly strong in the tenth where it is accidentally dignified.

For vocational rewards, a career for the sake of more and more material gain, prestige, or power alone will never satisfy these people, no matter how outwardly successful they may appear. There is restlessness, or that ever-nagging suspicion that they are being overlooked, or in danger of it. A life work that challenges the mind, lets creative juices flow, or uses the fertile imagination is where these people will find the particular benefits they desire.

If the chart is business-oriented, motivation must be toward bettering a service given, delegating duties that bring out the mind or the creative force or initiative in others, developing greater excellence if there is a product and keeping it honestly priced, and conscientiously living up to claims of quality. This is as opposed to quantity or profit. These people must have come to terms with themselves regarding compromises that must be made in order to achieve greater profits. Although acceptable business-wise, these compromises may nevertheless be improper in the ethical sense. Such businesses as book stores, art supply houses, or anything that supports the arty or creative demand or tastes, can be unusually successful. Service or artistic motivation, intellectual or imaginative release, or dealing with the unusual makes the difference between success and failure.

There are some who may pursue two careers in the event that one fails. But, significantly enough, the second will be a service career or a creative outlet through which to express originality; the latter would bring greater satisfaction.

The parent of the same sex whose unusually strong personality (subtle or direct, depending on other factors in the chart) or the loss or neglect of this parent has a powerful motivating influence on these people as children toward later fulfilling ambitions and expectations. Later the strong vocational self-projection can be a direct outcome of this.

Those with Lilith in the tenth must be more dedicated to the spirit of their profession—its goals and ideals—and the intellectual, creative, or spiritual growth from it they can express or bring out in others, rather than for selfish gain. Then they will find Lilith to be a dependable guide to success, both professionally and as a socially contributing human being. As a result they are often considered to be an authority, unique, or special in some way in their field. Among writers with Lilith in the tenth are astrologers Grant Lewi, Elbert Benjamine, and Llewellyn George. In the field of entertainment are Marion Davies, Pat O'Brien, and Carol Burnett (see chart 10). Burnett's Lilith in Capricorn, also accidentally dignified in the tenth, brings great success to her, having been not only the star of a long running variety show but an inspiration to those who worked for her and who often said she was the rock that held them all together. Midheaven ruler Jupiter in the sixth trine Lilith exemplifies the support, respect, and trust she attracted through an impersonal (Uranus in the first) and self-effacing manner (Pisces rising) that always kept her genuinely concerned for the greater success of her crew.

In the scientific world, Albert Einstein's chart has Lilith in the tenth conjunct Saturn, and Mercury in early Aries sextile Mars in late Capricorn and quincunx Uranus in Virgo (see chart 11). His total immersion in his work brought out the full promise of brilliance that Lilith in the tenth house offers to anyone dedicated to creative or technical achievement.

Lilith in the Eleventh House
People with Lilith in the eleventh house never totally feel they are a part of the group, and the purely mundane element in friendship has no real existence for them. There is nothing passive or personal about Lilith that can long be tolerated without uneasy feelings of being overshadowed arising. However, within shared intellectual, creative, or otherwise impersonally involved activities that circumvent the emotional ego, they are indeed the most supportive, helpful, and dynamically inspiring friends. Many times they will lead social functions with their electric personalities. They feel extraordinarily confident with, and have a strong affinity for, those whose mind or talents they respect, can learn from, teach, or contribute to. These people are unusually

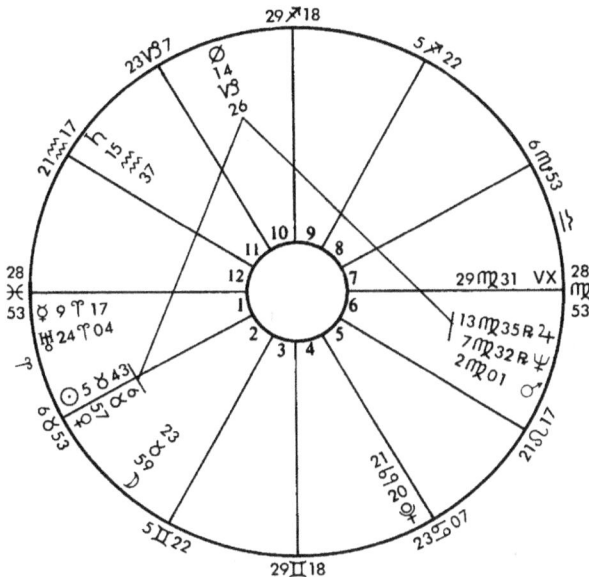

Chart 10. Carol Burnett, April 26, 1933, 4:15 a.m., San Antonio, Texas; source: B.C. per Penfield

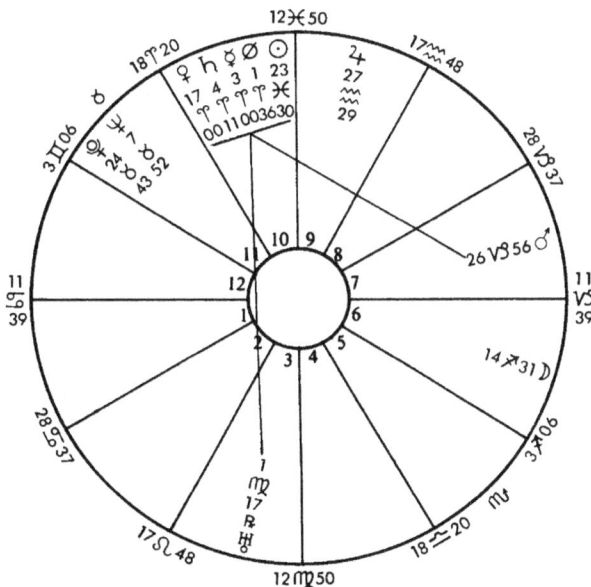

Chart 11. Albert Einstein, March 14, 1879, 11:30 a.m., Ulm Wurttemberg, Germany; source: Wemyss and Gauquelin

bright, socially sensitive, and inventive, when impersonal.

On the other hand, if these people cannot depersonalize in friendship—in other words, forget about themselves, Lilith creates anxious feelings of being ignored or faceless. This leads to personality conflicts, anxiety, insecurity, and an often resented sense of social inferiority, particularly in their early social orientation. On this level they can be petulant, hostile, or resentful, and some are trouble makers. All in all, very tricky to deal with and given to outbursts that seem to make no sense. Ask their friends.

They feel denied of the sympathetic understanding, personal recognition, or appreciation they need (not unlike a child) to reassure themselves of their security with people. The effect is quite the opposite. If these people are selfish or look for any kind of ego gratification in friendship or in group activities, no matter how justified they feel in deserving it, they will only attract the same selfish expectations from others and be frustrated. Lilith is an impersonal vibration, period. It consistently only supports (or forces) detachment within social relationships. Satisfaction will come only when they get lost in what is going on and forget about themselves. It is then that they are overwhelmingly accepted. Lilith is extreme one way or the other.

In the eleventh house Lilith signifies where critically needed objectivity is to be developed, and sharing of non-personal activities, intellectual interests, vocational aspirations, and spiritual or creative goals must be the basis of friendship and group endeavors. These people have a blind spot, otherwise, that accounts for an incredible sensitivity, as those close to them can testify. Nothing else will do because nothing else will distract them from themselves. They are too subjective otherwise (which they secretly abhor), emotionally self-centered, or surprisingly naive with people, becoming hurt and upset (or upsetting) when personal feelings leave them feeling strangely denied. These people feel deeply overshadowed by others' personalities, consciously or not. On the one hand, they may seek constant attention for themselves and their problems, and on the other, overcompensate for their sensitivity with sudden bombastic behavior that appears erratic or rude, but which, in reality, actually stems from a resentful or prideful defensiveness.

Lilith rules the intellectual soul. Because of the totally impersonal/universal/social nature of the planet, it clearly represents frustration, disppointment, or blanket denial for emotional personalization in the house it motivates. In this case, it is within eleventh house matters and these relationships. Lilith is anathema to sentiment or human weakness. It indicates, when negative, where naivete or foolish expectancies are the Achilles Heel. In the eleventh, these people, although intolerant of others, surprisingly demand and expect not only tolerance for themselves but total support and appreciation. The resulting disillusionment from the denials they face will force the greater realism they need to elevate the desire nature. No apologies are made for Lilith. It is as impersonally demanding of emotional maturation (gnowing up) as Saturn is for mature organization and responsibility in the house it tenants.

The personal detachment that Lilith calls for with people, through the sharing of intellectual, educational, esthetic, creative, or group goals, allows only these higher attitudes to create a successful atmosphere for understanding that would be totally aside from personality approval or disapproval. Within it each can work and speak more freely, give and take suggestions and enjoy what becomes an incredibly stimulating social experience in pursuit of respective goals. Strictly professional fields of interest, importantly, create the nondependence emotionally that allows for objectivity to rise. They need it to develop and maintain mature social expression. Within such mutual support, Lilith generates an incredible closeness with friends, not to mention a super charm in groups that attracts devoted followers and students alike. Indeed, Lilith magnifies persuasiveness and success where there is depersonalization, and frustrates personal ego. Problems here would indicate the latter is taking place, no matter how it is justified or made to look the opposite.

Even in the most positive individuals, during times when the nonpersonal breaks down, the feeling of being cancelled out or unappreciated may spark the sudden rude behavior, petulance, or a defeatist attitude. It may be all three (characteristic of negative Lilithian behavior) in direct contrast to their impersonal objective side, where they are so amazingly self-sustaining, supportive, fascinating, and respected. Lilith is this kind of an enigma, and can earn for the native a reputation for being eccentric. Friends do not really appreciate hearing about their personal problems. In fact, they are rather surprised at the sudden reversal it seems to be, or the immaturity it seems to expose in their makeup—which it is. They may even understand, but do not know what the Lilith person wants. They will listen, but in the bargain become uncomfortable with their inability to handle things. They may either flatly and firmly tell them what they could constructively do, or failing this, politely pander to the ego until they can get away, because at a time like this these people do not really want advice. They just want assurances of what fine people they are. Having Lilith in the eleventh brings the Lilith in others toward them. Lacking the ability to detach themselves from the ego at this time and take themselves a little less seriously can make them unexpectedly unnerving when their personal anxieties take over, which they can do quite suddenly for no apparent reason to others.

Wherever Lilith denies the individual an ego security blanket (and deny, it will) is where one's own selfish expectations correlate to self-undoing. In the eleventh house, Lilith magnifies any weaknesses with people. Professionally, when this is displayed, it lowers the value to superiors who fear taking a chance on the individual's ability to get along with others, no matter how brilliant he or she is otherwise—an important eleventh house consideration.

In one case, a woman with a Ph.D. in education had a superior work evaluation under which she applied for tenure at the university where she was head of the educational department. However, her interdepartmental relationships were termed irresponsible by the board of evaluations and she was turned down. Her eleventh house Lilith is in Leo conjunct the North Node and square Saturn in Scorpio and Sun in Taurus. Always fearing that her job security was being undermined, fellow teachers often found it impossible to deal with her opinionated ideas and overdramatic behavior, even though she was exceptional otherwise. She was considered a trouble maker.

It may sound contradictory that when impersonal this woman could be at her excellent best and a crack administrator, but when personalities entered in she could be intimidating or unreasonable. People with this placement are capable of such extremes, and thus the respect of a friend can be abruptly lost or shaken by an incredibly badly timed remark or letter. They can astound others instantly when an innocent observation comes too close to the person's insecurities. Judgment is strengthened only from the sophistication these people gains through depersonalization: in other words, just forgetting about themselves. These people also have an elevated desire for what they hope to gain from their life's work.

Generous, supportive efforts for another's creative, spiritual, or intellectual growth is one of their most beautiful social expressions. It is where they can shine most magnetically. These people have an absolutely fascinating way with others and are able to draw out talents as no one else can. They just seem to know what others can do, imbuing a confidence previously never felt possible. Those with Lilith in the eleventh house can be prime movers of people once they let go of themselves. The victory is in the letting go. When this is done through a philosophical live and let live attitude, or a selflessly spiritual approach to people, they become special people indeed and a source of inspiration to the group. Strangely enough, among those they support they will find many of their own teachers, not to mention sincere appreciation, and respect that creates deeper friendships than they would have known otherwise.

If in advanced adulthood they are still experiencing frustration in friendships, be assured that self-centeredness, conscious or not, is contributing to it. This is not uncommon until they replace their emotional dependence on friends, for impersonal interests with friends. After all, we attract experiences to live through that mirror our own attitudes. To avoid being judged difficult to deal with, these people should analyze situations from a logical or pragmatic viewpoint and come to fair and impersonal conclusions. This brings you credibility and a positive interest in your ideas from others.

With stepchildren and sons- and daughters-in-law, it is creative rapport or intellectual appreciation of each other that must be established, a meeting of the minds as friends might share, for the younger one to ever feel that he or she has been accepted. They cannot relate to the Lilith person on the ordinary family level because they are too liable to feelings of inferiority or fear of being overshadowed. It is important to respect that these people have a right to their own ways and opinions, just as does the Lilith person, and to establish a communication to really get to know one another better. Then the Lilith person will find these young people to be fascinating individuals from whom, surprisingly, a great deal can eventually be learned. These people are often unusually bright, but have trouble adjusting socially to people, starting with the Lilith individual, who could bring out a talent through which a beautifully shared relationship arises that is securely based on understanding and a respect that allows for differences.

Lilith in the Twelfth House
Lilith in this natural house of Neptune exaggerates ideals, receptivity, and whatever is the level of sensitivity in this one's makeup. In the twelfth house Lilith sensitizes the native to deep wells of etheric energy, accounting for an extraordinary imagination when positive, and illusion or self-delusion when negative. When positive, there are products of a beautifully creative imagination. This indicates sensitivity for work with color or shading, denoting artistic talent if the rest of the chart is supportive. There is ability for work with intangibles such as energy fields, either as a scientist or mystic depending upon the chart, or with the delicate nuances of sound or rhythm as in the case of a musician or dancer. It may be metaphysics or the paranormal. They

can act on stage or in film because they can convincingly identify with a fictional role due to the unusual ability to relate easily to the world of the imagination.

These people have a deep mystical awareness they may choose not to admit, or deny in themselves, because of what they secretly fear they cannot handle, that might separate them from others; or invite rejection. It creates an unusually strong inner life—one that is particularly out of proportion within self-centered orientation. When selfishly motivated (justified or not), or where the emotions are undisciplined or misdirected, Lilith's higher level of inspirational guidance is denied positive outlet because it is entirely foreign to the negative desire nature and therefore debilitating. It is hostile to the desires of the flesh, where these people are apt to deify their own desires and blind themselves to whatever may deny them. The visionary quality then becomes distorted. The Lilith energy buildup, releasing through no detachment or personal objectivity to make it independent of the emotional, turns in on itself to literally blind the native to certain facts. This causes serious self-defeating errors in their judgment. Lilith in the twelfth house magnifies illusion to unhealthy levels when the quality of detachment is lacking.

There is a kind of naivete about those who have Lilith in the twelfth that invites deception. They believe what they idealize to be true, and no amount of alerting them to certain facts seems to help. They leave themselves open to deception by ignoring signals along the way because of an almost childlike optimism. This is suspected by those close to them, but it is amazing to those who only see their deliberate outer composture. Their super-imagination unreleased through higher lines of the mind, a vocation, or a positive expression of themselves works instead to fantasize. It makes the illusion as concrete a reality to them as a stone fence might be to another. To say that they can be naive on the emotional level is a masterpiece of understatement. They seem to have an incredible mental block where their personal realities are concerned. On this level their otherwise good judgment is as if paralyzed when the threat of upset is in the wind. Love and affection mean too much to them, so what they cannot face they simply consider nonexistent, and that's that.

You might say these people inspired the phrases "burying one's head in the sand" and "what you don't know can't hurt you." When finally awakened to the hard realities—in other words, disillusioned—they feel not only betrayed but brutally awakened. They become as disoriented as might be the case when a sleeping person is awakened by someone suddenly turning on all the lights while shouting. Lilith's rapid negative action does not debilitate as much as it exposes an already debilitating situation. Hopefully this injects some perspective into the makeup for having had the experience. A false situation or relationship may have gone on for many years, the disillusionment of which marks a profound change in the personality. The fear of believing in anything again has the hardening effect they need. Depending on the rest of the chart, these people may then compensate with more healthy suspicion in the future, which they need in order to avoid self-defeating situations.

Lilith's difficult shake-ups are simply the result of a Pollyannalike attitude that blinds objectivity in the personal life. Lilith exposes the individual to painful but maturing reality in order to further a critically needed personal redefinement. These people need to view or deal with their lives through the more pragmatic eyes of the intellect (a logical view) to establish sufficient detachment from the overactive imagination and to balance it. Until they really want to do this, and even though they may be outstanding in other ways, they are capable of immersing themselves comfortably, if naively, in the dream of what a certain person or situation should represent, rather than the facts. Though they may find it hard to admit, apparently even to themselves, they are deeply apprehensive of their ability to cope with mundane realities. They prefer to lose themselves to their great preoccupation with love and ideals. So these people work hard to display an outer composure that says, "Things are just fine." Eventually it becomes so automatic that it becomes a part of them.

So long as a personal situation serves their purpose they can completely close their eyes to what they do not wish to see, and let it go at that. Can you see how they can be taken advantage of? It is an amazing thing to observe even though they can otherwise be discriminating in the more impersonal areas of their lives. There seems to be no logic as to why they will tolerate certain personal situations.

Of course, all twelfth house Liliths do not necessarily react in this way. Much depends upon the rest of the chart and particularly on whether there are enough positive signatures to help them rise above misplaced trust (naivete) through a natural mental or creative bent. When there are qualities of detachment in the chart or the ability to be objective, the negative is transcended earlier in life or more swiftly brought into perspective. When positive, we have the sensitive or visionary person who can become immersed in areas that productively or impersonally channel the sensitivity for the greater release of their fertile imagination—actors, artists, dancers, writers, inventors, technologists, or those involved in work that satisfies the creative imagination. At the very least there is something of the dreamer in all of them.

There is nothing halfway about Lilith. Whereas Lilith may be accursed in the twelfth to the selfish dream, in an equal and opposite way, it is pure inspiration to artistic/social desire. Lilith is a clear avenue for truth, beauty, and satisfaction within the higher values of the mind or creative and vocational talents.

Where Lilith is located the victory is in the letting go, and in this case, of self-serving dreams. Lilithian energy is only debilitating when denied.

In severe cases where these people cannot or will not detach, the eventual uprooting from their false dreams may reverse the too trusting attitude into an unhealthy bitterness, escape into secret indulgences, or personality distortions as a result of having had their rose-colored glasses removed. It leaves them feeling stripped naked from their comfortable illusions and exposed to a chilling world. In this case the negative attitude may create illness, confinement, a wasted life, or simply another illusion in which to comfortably wrap themselves. This only delays the inevitable awakening for another disillusionment. It is not Lilith that is static as much as it is the desire to "hide in the dream" that is their own self-undoing. One day when they are forced to face the reality of the situation (however it occurs), they will have to admit they did use it to avoid certain decisions as much as it or a person used them. The problem seems sudden, but the handwriting was on the wall to all but themselves.

Those with Lilith in the twelfth deeply need the inspiration of an artistic, imaginative environment. It can result from their own esthetic efforts in decorating their homes, or from surrounding themselves with an unspoiled view of nature. They could lose themselves in meditation for a time in order to escape the real world, as if to refresh the soul. They need this as much as another might need rest and relaxation for the body. It essentially satisfies their need and their strong affinity for the delicate or the idyllic, which is actually the greater reality to them. They need refreshment for the soul from things esthetic as urgently as others need refrshment from food and drink. It helps them to get or maintain their emotional perspective and detachment from themselves—personal balance. Given these nourishments, there exist some of the most creatively sensitive artists and intelligent scientists (material or occult) because of the tremendous insight and feeling Lilith makes these people heir to in the twelfth house.

Where vocations are concerned, the actors or actresses among them make excellent use of the exaggerated imaginative factor of Lilith in the twelfth. It is a particularly wealthy source to draw from in their work of visualizing a reality other than their own. They can forget themselves completely in order to relate to the unreality of a fictional character. Rather than a weakness, it becomes their strength as the capacity to believe for a time that they are in fact the character they portray, enabling them to lose themselves in it. There is great satisfaction for them in any area of the entertainment world or related fields, where they can deliciously let their imagination go its limit. So too in the art world, where what they envision is the inspiration that drives them in their work and satisfies.

In the theatre, within detachment to their work, Lilith heightens charisma, memory, and the reflective quality needed to temporarily make real something unreal. Here they can work with illusion as a tool of their trade, keeping the reality and the unreality clearly defined and thus in good balance. Among such artists were charismatic film star Joseph Cotton, and Greta Garbo, who began her career as a dancer (see chart 12). Garbo was a widely admired and respected professional in her work. She has Lilith exalted in Gemini conjunct Pluto square a fifth house Sun in Virgo and sextile Venus in Leo. She became one of the most celebrated actresses the screen has ever known, and her films are considered classics. In her personal life she was well known for her illusiveness from the press and her intense dislike of publicity. She considered her profession just that and nothing more. She gave up acting in 1941 at the peak of her career without any explanation.

In Garbo's chart, Lilith is well placed by sign in the twelfth house, conjoining the loner tendencies, perfectionism, and guarded privacy of Pluto, magnified by conjunction, and square the Sun. It explains not only the extremes of her career—at one point world celebrated and at another abruptly dropped from sight, but also the extreme of co-operating fully for publicity in her professional life while having total abhorence and complete refusal for it in her private one.

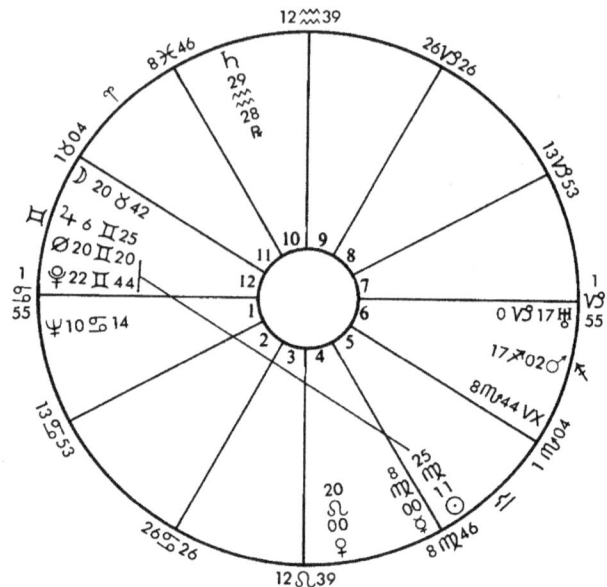

Chart 12. Greta Garbo, September 18, 1905, 9:00 p.m., Stockholm, Sweden; source: Church of Light

The exaggerated sensitivity of Lilith on this level, for those with Lilith in the twelfth, was simply translated into an incredible veil over her comings and goings. She had lived her life since then in total obscurity from the press, and had become a celebrated mystery woman. While Pluto accounts in large part for the mystery, Lilith accounts for the legend.

Howard Hughes, on the other hand, had Lilith square a retrograde Neptune in the fourth, the natal as well as natural ruler of his twelfth. It created the similar exaggerated desire for secrecy and utter abhorence of publicity. He, as Garbo, eventually became a complete recluse (see chart 13 on page 113). Although Lilith was not in his twelfth, this example is used to demonstrate a similar effect when it heavily aspects Neptune or the twelfth house ruler. In his case it did both. He succumbed to it in his later life as Neptune ruling the twelfth was in the fourth, depicting that period. The digression was to make a point for the similiarity of the in-house position and Lilith's eventual effect on a house by strong aspect to its ruler.

When capable of spiritual objectivity, people with Lilith in the twelfth can be instrumental in inspiring others through their emphasis on selfless ideals and mystical beliefs (Meher Baba/mystic). If the chart supports it, they can be excellent in healing work, as in Charles H. Mayo, founder of one of the world's largest medical institutions, the Mayo Clinic. There was the incredible genius vision of Werner Von Braun, an aeronautical engineer who, upon realizing his dream of rocketry and missiles in Germany, was frustrated through the Nazi downfall in World War II, and simply switched alliances to the U.S. He wanted to continue his work undisturbed and was unfettered by decisions of allegiance. To him, it was the dream (in other words, what he envisioned) that must go on, regardless of where.

Chapter 5

Aspects to Lilith

When interpreting aspects to Lilith, keep in mind its specialized level. Remember that it distorts or frustrates the intentions for emotional or ego satisfaction, no matter how innocent or justified they may seem. Lilith is foreign to selfish desire. It is successful and inspiring only to mentally stimulating, creative, or spiritual desire; in other words, for the impersonal, whether it be in relationships or what you do. Basically, Lilith represents the social-universal instincts, and denies anything that is not socially creative, intellectual, service-oriented, or selfless.

Trine and Sextile
Trines and sextiles from Lilith may not necessarily indicate the personally supportive circumstances, emotional comforts, or opportunities these aspects would ordinarily indicate. Lilith is nonreflective (denying) to these superficial levels. However, they do indicate where people are more capable of an earlier adjustment to its personal denials and can develop the needed detachment. What I am saying is that, in this case, early frustrating experiences in the house of Lilith may mature one more rapidly. He or she may stumble on the higher way at which to operate through the process of trial and error, or through wise advice from the positive Lilithian types these aspects to Lilith will bring him into contact with. As with Saturn aspects, however, he can accept it as a fact of life, or he can reject it. The choice is his, which may (or may not) be influenced by other planets that affect the one Lilith is aspecting. If he will accept his personal limitations here, then the harmonies these aspects represent are forthcoming in great power.

Lilith liberates one from subjectivity when attitudes are positive, but distinctly eliminates happiness when they are negative (self-serving). The type of aspect certainly helps, but it is the *level* of motivation or intention that makes the essential difference. Lilith is simply exaggerating the need here for greater impersonality, detachment, or intellectuality in order to successfully handle the house affairs the planet represents. After all, it must be in *some* area of life experience that we evolve to, or live in, a greater social maturity. This is simply the one. Aspects in themselves are not necessarily good or bad. They are simply the yardstick of energy by which we measure the particular degree of force between two planets. The square family of aspects may very well indicate the same degree of talent as the trine family, but they are in more critical need of development, there are important obstacles to be overcome due to the station or background of life, or there are greater problems in manifesting these talents due to character faults the planet Lilith is magnifying by aspect.

Square and Opposition
Squares and oppositions are more difficult of course because ordinarily it is not in the nature of the individual to be impersonal here. They will be insidiously denying unless or until these people can finally let go of their self-preoccupation—and with it some naive expectations, sentimentality, or comfortable security blankets—and surrender their will to the higher forces of the mind, the spirit, or the creative imagination. Through it they develop new resolve. This releases special talents that can then surface through the Lilith aspect.

For the naturally detached individual, the hard angles may show so severe an impersonality as to earmark a genius factor because of the positive forces of the mind Lilith can then bring forward. In this case it may actually be the basis for an incredible talent. Nevertheless, within the personal-emotional life it indicates critical blind-spots that these people must continually guard against or periods of false security. Strange as it may seem, with the hard angles you may see one who is as wise in some areas as the proverbial owl, but so incredibly blind when personality or emotional static clouds the issue so as to become open to being shamelessly taken advantage of. The Lilith principal of impersonality being denied, it then denies clear thinking and strangely distorts the logic. The house matters involved demand a rational approach, and until these people can accept that it is *their* responsibility to create such an atmosphere here, the problem continues. The lesson learned is one in emotional perspective—or it will be. With this in mind I will offer my findings for the reader to investigate in the hope that through it another door is opened for the greater use of Lilith in chart delineation.

Aspects from the Sun
Lilith conjunct the Sun or in the same sign as the Sun magnifies to a more than usually noticeable degree the basic solar qualities, interests, or talents. It magnifies willfulness and adds a certain distinction to the individual that makes him or her stand out from others.

In opposition, Lilith forces emotional perspective and individuality through relationships, and focuses more strongly in the makeup the qualities of the sign opposing the Sun—its polarity. For instance, if the Sun is in Taurus opposed by Lilith, the loner tendencies of Scorpio are sharply noticeable, and there is more extremism in the makeup of this particular Taurus Sun person.

In the fourth sign square from the Sun, Lilith generates a distinct difference from the rest of the family, and something unusual about the parent of the opposite sex. When positive, it may be that the parent is a person of letters or unusual talent. In a negative chart, it may indicate denial of the parent (or from the parent) in some manner to the native, or an extremely difficult relationship.

In the tenth sign, square from the Sun, it focuses ambition and a heavy career thrust.

The Sun in close aspect or conjunct Lilith gives strong presence and an indomitable will. This one is a strong individualist, make no mistake about that, who, while not particularly trying to outshine others, must maintain a uniqueness. They cannot abide comparison of themselves to others and prefer that each person—including themselves—stand in their own light. Although the appearance may be given, depending upon the chart, they cannot entirely yield their will to the group for long without an inner nagging discomfort building up. It will sooner or later erupt into actions or words that finally relieve them from the shadow they feel placed in by the ego of another, even if it is self-defeating. It may appear to have come from nowhere and is irritatingly puzzling, if not maddening, to those around them. It is not so much an independence that they seek as much as it is the right to be different that they must satisfy within themselves, and have it recognized by others. They understand criticism if it is based on what they do from an impersonal point of view, but never because of what others expect of them. In the latter case they can be totally impossible, as if the divine right of kings were being dared to be denied them. On the emotional level they can be as egotistical as they can be kind, and thus they can be graciously humble when dealing with impersonal factors. Lilith brings out the extreme on either level.

For one reason or another these people are prominent and can be the loyalest of friends if no one tries to dominate them. Quite the contrary, the latter brings out an omniscience in them that will, depending upon the chart, either make them cut others out of their life even though, or suddenly react with an abrupt or even cruel action that banishes others from their presence for all practical purposes. They attract the extremes of feelings from others—either to admire and follow them, or to go to great lengths to avoid their strangely scorching presence.

As people with Lilith-Uranus aspects would need the freedom of future associations to look forward to (to keep their options open, you might say), those with Lilith-Sun aspects not only need but reserve the right to individually or creatively express and do what they will, and to shine or fall as long as it is in their own particular way. In many instances they tend to attract others who seem to dog their footsteps until they forget about themselves enough and their attitudes (depersonalize) to successfully rise above it and continue on their way to greater creative output. It is as if they were challenged for their place in the Sun. Otherwise, they are constantly put in a position of sharing honors with others. It is a humbling experience, but they need it for greater emotional perspective and objectivity.

When it comes to children they are not so much involved with their physical or emotional care and development (beyond what is necessary) as much as they are with the intellectual or creative development of their charges. This is not to say that their parental duties are not properly seen to. It would depend on other factors in the chart. This is merely to say that they primarily relate through encouraging greater individuality in others to be the best they can be where their mind and/or talents are concerned. Without such communication there are problems with children and young people.

Particularly with the trine or sextile, they make excellent teachers in the literary or esthetic arts. They have a deep sense of the drama of life and, as those around them can tell you, play each role they accept in life to the hilt as if the world were a stage and each person in it a key player. Unless indications elsewhere in the chart inhibit it, they keenly respect and will personally support any creative expression is different, encouraging others to be stars in their own right. This is not to say that anyone else is better, but that each person has the right to be himself or herself, whatever that may be. They can be a great inspiration to others in bringing out individuality and creative effort when they believe in someone. They will share themselves unstintingly (depending on the sign the Sun is in) if the individual choice of expression runs along a different line, even slightly, but they are distinctly uncomfortable if they feel duplicated. They will nevertheless avoid open competition because they feel themselves above this sort of thing, and believe more in *noblesse oblige* rather than believe there could be another like them. Leadership drive is strong and always kept as a personal option.

Of course with the hard angles, when attitudes are negative or naive, egotistical tendencies may be noted because the self-importance is then crassly exaggerated in the makeup by Lilith. They become impressed with themselves. In this case they can be sporadically dominating to those who will not bend to their will. But in areas that circumvent the personal ego, they are incredibly magnanimous and talented, as the hard angles give a surplus of positive energy when maturely directed. The need is to depersonalize in order to handle the sophistication of Lilith that brings out an enormous creative potential.

Aspects from the Moon
The connections between Lilith and the Moon would at first seem to indicate a contradictory nature or personality inconsistencies, because in influence they are so opposite to one another: the

Moon indicates the personalizing of the self and Lilith indicates the depersonalizing of the self. However, this need not necessarily be difficult. Between them they describe the two separate but necessary sides to a well balanced personality. Ideally, the trine would describe a well integrated desire nature between the dependent emotional needs and responses of the native (Moon), and the independent urges of the socially oriented, intellectual, or creative-social side of the nature (Lilith); in other words, between the personal and the impersonal makeup. The personal life as opposed to outside vocational involvement (or areas that circumvent the personal ego), are usually better defined as to who the individual is in both and what he or she can reasonably expect in both. This is, of course, barring harsh aspects to the Moon or Lilith. For a woman there is a natural gravitation to creative, social, or career interests that are aside from her personal life in which both needs can be satisfied but in different ways.

In the case of the conjunction, one woman with this aspect in the first house solved the dilemma quite nicely by adopting a completely different name for her business personality. This satisfied her need for an independent identity and expressed the liberated more worldly side of her nature; in this case, the impersonal business woman running a successful clothing shop dependent on no one but her own enterprise. The sextile would indicate the same personality balance as the trine, except that it must be deliberately sought through an outside activity; intellectual interest, or a creative expression of herself somehow, if a housewife. If a career woman, it may be through family, marriage involvement, or the like. This one must make the effort to diversify her horizons in either direction, in order to include the personal-emotional desires of the Moon for satisfaction in one area of their life, and the impersonal, creative or independent satisfactions in another.

With the opposition aspect, the emotional makeup (Moon) appears to attract conditions or relationships that are in conflict with furthering their emotional maturing needs (Lilith). The emotional dependencies and desires must be finely balanced by independent, impersonal, or job interests, or at least shared for some mutual goal. If not, relationships suffer. For example, if the Moon is in Libra opposition Lilith in Aries, the emotional need for harmony in relationships may seriously frustrate their initiative and courage to move directly on what they believe in. They might try to block the strong self-assertiveness of Lilith in Aries in order to avoid upsets, and then inwardly build up strong resentment for having no say in things. In this case, the Lilith energy would distort the Libra Moon not as much toward indecisiveness as much as toward sudden contradictory behavior that seems completely and for no apparent reason out of character. Being denied, Lilith would deny any sense of emotional peace. This will eventually create sudden breaks in relationships as a result of the nagging fear these people cannot shake when they feel they have no rights of their own.

This accounts for the sudden declaration of independence or the seemingly cruel periods of separativeness that seem to come out of nowhere as far as others are concerned. They see only the outer cooperative passive nature for long periods of time. Although the about face deliciously releases their tension or resentment buildup, it creates serious personal relationship problems they must solve by letting go of their emotional security blanket of "peace at any price" and realize the price may be too high. They must divide themselves equally between their relationship needs and an independent area of interest that is strictly their own. This pretty much goes for any two signs involved in an opposition as this aspect always indicates two opposite poles of energy that one must balance with diversified interest between one's own needs and that of another.

In square, the emotional nature is in contrast to the instinctive thought processes, or it could be said that the personal needs work at cross purposes to the creative expressional needs. The extremes of the two sides appear at different times, according to activation. Nevertheless, the friction indicates a powerfully focused emotional nature, creating strong mediumistic tendencies and public appeal but also an eccentric defensiveness against any personal intrusions or confrontations they might suspect. These people must find a way to give equal time to both areas or else an emotional imbalance occurs, bursting forth and unexpectedly overwhelming the native. Depending on the chart it may create a suspicious and sometimes devious nature because of their magnified feelings of subjectivity to others (Richard Nixon). This may account for subtly intimidating ways if they suspect bad weather ahead, making others uneasy, as if being maneuvered. In less aggressive charts it may simply manifest by their discreetly keeping themselves separated from any areas they suspect may upset them, offering no explanation. This is not to say that they cannot be brilliant, but the square interferes with or at times flatly negates their ability to think clearly. It is as if they must ride it out this way.

The Lilith-Moon square may exaggerate early emotional dependencies that seriously stunt their all-around maturity, creating periods of severe despondency (Marilyn Monroe), particularly if either planet is in the fourth house. There may be too much self-identification with or dependency or sensitivity to the mother's relationship or appraisal of the individual. These people must clearly establish independence and come to terms emotionally with some early family difficulty or difference from other families. They must establish their priorities between the family they develop as adults, their adult home or personal life, and the impersonal-vocational life. If not, in one or the other they become so fiercely anxious about those who might deny, reject, or misunderstand them as to have it create major problems in relationships, or manifest as emotional or health breakdowns.

If their work is in one of the fields that has Cancer rulership, or they are in something else where they deal directly with the public in which they take can take full advantage of their intellectual ability or creative initiative, they are better able to successfully release their emotionally based energies successfully. People with Lilith-Moon aspects can be very appealing to the public because they have the unusual ability to identify with public trends. However, it is important that their personal feelings or selfish desires be strictly separated from practical considerations in work; otherwise, there will be too much preoccupation with self that interferes with concentration and creates major problems with others in the career. Depending on the chart they may have to deal with this in other people. Hopefully, through the experience (or experiences) they will gain perspective on their own powerful defensive reactions by recognizing this sensitivity and selfish preoccupation in others.

In all cases the home is very important. It must be emotionally comfortable for those who are there so the native can be emotionally comfortable with them. When positive, this manifests as a gracious host or hostess who sees to everyone's comforts. It becomes so much of an unconscious effort (defense mechanism) that it appears entirely natural to others—everyone, that is, except the perceptive few. Those who would frustrate the atmosphere these people set may not at first realize the polite maneuverings that transform matters to more comfortable emotional limits. If they cannot do this, others will soon come up against a surprising hostility. There is no intention to be dishonest in their hospitality, but rather it is to simply protect themselves against possible inroads they fear they cannot emotionally handle.

Aspects from Mercury
Lilith-Mercury aspects produce so lively an imagination that these people can mentally journey back to areas previously covered, and can zoom in for a closer view of things or persons they want to see more clearly. They can lose themselves in savoring the minutest details, and the mind is always moving somewhere, restless until it can settle on something to occupy its attention. They are readers and storers of information. When positive in their logic it produces some of the most dynamic teachers and writers (Manly Palmer Hall, Marc Edmund Jones, and Dane Rudhyar).

The mind likes to wander into the future. It brings back ideas to share or develop, or it wanders to distant places where there is someone they want to talk with, having as active a mental conversation with them as if they were together and the space between them inconsequential. The mind likes to roam in search of information or to revisit a place that remains interesting. The scene becomes so vivid in the mind as to evoke perfectly clear mental pictures of themselves with others, down to the feelings of joy in being back and all the sites down to the last detail. It is not just remembering, but revisiting to wander down streets and continue conversations.

Through the vivid imagination the mind can also literally journey ahead to preempt its impressions for arrival at a distant place. These people may be apt to question the why of something that may be different even though they were not expecting anything in particular. They wonder why things look strangely familiar when they are not. They may be surprised as to the changes they see that they like or dislike and may wonder about previous knowledge of the location. Thoughts might be: "I haven't been here before so why am I so thrilled at finally rounding out a picture of something I am first now seeing?" This combination can often be found in people who say, "I must have been here before but not to my knowledge." This implies strong psychic impressions or extra sensory perception.

If people with Lilith-Mercury aspects are involved in a conversation that does not hold their interest, the mind is off on something else that is more interesting while at the same time appearing to be totally involved in every spoken word. This is not to be insincere, but merely to avoid being rude. They will extricate themselves from the situation as soon as possible unless the personal comes into it and evokes strong feelings. In this case the emotional static deadens the imagination and they are apt to lock themselves into the conversation as if fearing a mental desert without it, becoming repetitious and boring—the same thing they flee from in others. Lilith is only positive on impersonal levels. So unless the exchange is free and informative without personal invasion or boredom, it begins to negate the mental clarity and they will (if positive) choose to be silent; if negative, it will begin to sound like a phonograph needle stuck in the same groove. The conversation goes nowhere and they hate themselves for it afterward. This is much like Lilith in the third house.

When selfishly or superficially oriented (negative), Lilith distorts the logic and frustrates the ability to concentrate, even sometimes to the point of negating the ability to speak clearly. When positive, and particularly if Mercury is well aspected to Neptune, it can indicate a photographic memory or clairaudience. Ordinarily these are college educated or exquisitely self-taught people. There is an unusually strong curiosity, but only in subjects that catch their fancy. Otherwise, they are irritated by details given on something they are not interested in. There is a high degree of intelligence when they can sufficiently extricate themselves from personal considerations. Credibility is important to them. They may hear themselves uttering information they have never researched. There is a certainty for the information's correctness. Through it they promptly learn something they never knew they knew before, as if there were a teacher inspiring the knowledge—and indeed there is. Many times they give the credit elsewhere rather than experience another's doubt.

Aspects from Venus
When Lilith is conjunct or in close aspect to Venus, the individuality can never be totally surrendered in relationships, although that impression may be given and even given enthusiastically. This is not as insincere as it may sound. At the time it is well meant and they are exceptionally accommodating; but they promptly detach when they part. Ordinarily this is not their intention at all. The first is simply an exaggeration of their social sensitivity, and the second is simply the end of it. They can appear totally related to a situation or interested in the person they are temporarily in contact with in one way while at the same time being detached from the whole thing in another. They are impersonally involved and gracious, but not personally involved and affected. They do truly care, make no mistake about that, but if the contact is one

they haven't any real interest in they simply do not take it seriously. However, if it is someone they have a strong interest in, they are among the most genuine people to be found for long-term cooperation. They are easily bored by the mundane in social contacts, avoid superficial involvements like the plague, and have a great capacity for enjoying their own company. Any overcompensation of interest in another, flattery, or an exaggerated sweetness and charm is a telltale effort of theirs to try to make a social contact work even though they would rather be somewhere else. Loving attention goes along with their grain for staying in a situation they feel is in reality wasting their time.

There is usually some artistic, literary, or musical talent if the native cares to pursue it and the chart supports it. Their values are not of the ordinary variety. This is usually noticeable in their choice of dress, spending habits, and/or pleasure. They can appear fickle, falling out of love easily or suddenly severing a relationship if they suspect their independence is being seriously threatened within it or because of it. They then feel as if they are being overshadowed and unfairly cancelled out, which they will not tolerate for long because of the exaggerated sense of their own personal worth, which they will surrender to no one.

Equality is magnified when Lilith aspects Venus, and these people can tolerate nothing less. The buildup toward a break in a relationship is never made noticeable. They will make every attempt to keep it intact as there is near reverence for cooperation. When convinced that it is impossible because of personality involvement, it is simply dropped with no explanation. This comes as a complete surprise to others who suspected nothing amiss because of the cooperative, romantic, or socially pleasant give and take displayed—until then. In any relationship their individuality must be kept intact while blending themselves with others. In friendships they will *not* be interfered with and expect to do as they please with no need for explanation. While they recognize the need for a cooperative spirit and very much need others for feedback, they abhor being swallowed up in a relationship. They must be free to make their own judgments.

In marriage there is devotion, as long as it does not prohibit their freedom to move among outside impersonal interests if they should choose to. This is not to be inconsiderate, which may or may not be the case elsewhere in the chart, but relationships are not so emotionally important that they will give up their freedom for long to interact with others as they choose. Relationships in which they can equalize themselves and strengthen their identity are very successful. Otherwise they won't hesitate to abruptly sever a relationship or leave it alone to die; having lost whatever it was that held it together may surprise and disappoint them. It is foolish to take these Lilith people for granted.

They are noticeable in the quality of lightness they bring to ordinary relationships, as if saying "you may come this close and no closer." This discourages overly personal attachments unless there is a seriously shared intellectual, creative interest or spiritual tie that binds them together.

In this case they are fascinating, helpful, and intelligent companions, and part of an incredibly successful relationship. Otherwise it is a case of out of sight, out of mind.

The trine between Lilith and Venus are supportive for more consistent success in artistic and literary endeavors, whereas with a square or opposition the creative talents may be greater, but their development and outlet is plagued with more difficulties or is only sporadically successful. Here, while the desire is just as strong if not stronger, something about the presentation is either out of step with the times or denied for lack of enough training. In negative charts, laziness or hiding one's light under a bushel is a tendency because although they do not seriously question their ability in something, they do paralyze their effort with doubt that others will accept it. If they can successfully detach and work relatively alone until they are ready, they can be infinitely more successful. Otherwise, there is much talk but no real accomplishment, as if waiting for someone to wipe away the doubt. They must learn to value the idea or the spirit of what they want to do rather than preoccupy themselves with the personal recognition they may get from it, or seek others' appreciation for it.

While marriage for them can be successful when Lilith is square Venus there are many separative situations they must learn to accept, or there is something separative they must adjust to in the makeup of the partner, which is probably what attracted them in the first place. This may hold true in the harmonious aspects also, but the adjustment is more comfortable.

Aspects from Mars
Mars in close aspect or conjunct lilith gives a strong personality. Whether it is subtly impressive or direct depends upon the rest of the chart, but it is always strongly assertive. These are people who are not easily ignored or overlooked for long. They are one of a kind. Originality, drive, and initiative are magnified. One can sense strength here, that although not always visible on the surface, is pervasive by the way in which they pursue their ideas or projects.

This combination magnifies ability for self-expression through decisive action. Anything less than decisive action makes them feel strangely vulnerable, uneasy, and fearful. During times like this they prefer behind-the-scenes activity, and cloak themselves in a kind of mystery or seeming nonparticipation.

Headstrong, they admire those who are direct, assertive, and independent, and are unstinting in their support of those who are singly battling to open the way for new ideas. There is something of the pioneer and loner in all of them, a strong sense of competition and fight, as you will soon learn if you try to challenge or thwart them for too long. There may be long periods of tolerance for those who would force their ways on them because there is secret admiration of such strength. However, when they have been pushed far enough they suddenly make an aggressive stand, much to the amazement of others who never suspected such hidden reserves.

In square or opposition aspect to Mars, Lilith can indicate hypertension, inflammation, or a propensity for accidents if either planet rules the first or sixth house, is aspected to one of their rulers, or is located in one of these houses. When unreleased along impersonal lines (apart from personalities), the energy frustrates the initiative, creating a tempermental disposition and abrupt temper. In stress aspect the native tends to act without forethought, as if defiantly, without consideration for the consequences or dangers. When the initiative is finally released along the higher lines of the intellect, the creative imagination, through compassion, or is otherwise impersonally channeled, their enterprise is nothing short of amazing.

Sexual magnetism is incredibly magnified, particularly if Mars is in the eighth house, as was the case with film stars Marilyn Monroe and Brigitte Bardot. People with Lilith-Mars aspects are often considered flirtatious, although this may or may not be their intent depending upon other factors in the chart. It is merely because they seek to know people underneath the outer facade, and thus their direct intense gaze is easily misread. You will notice this gaze if there is interest in you; otherwise you may feel a slight discomfort as if you're being tolerated.

When negative (Lilith's lower fear level), the ability of these people to make major decisions is frustrated, so that much time is spent spinning their wheels, They cannot seem to get started. They then see the competition exaggerated in their minds for what they want to do, so the preparations for new starts take on an incredible magnitude that leaves them in a state of exhaustion or depression, (everything must be perfect). Or they experience days long periods of wakefulness that leave their minds in no condition to make clear decisions. They must depersonalize (forget about themselves) or the perfectionistic tendencies of this combination will have them perpetually in a state of getting started but never getting started. Depending on the degree of sensitivity in the chart (Neptune's location and its aspects), they may be prone to self-defeat through substance abuse or any other form of escapism that serves to blot out the indecisiveness or stagnation associated with the guilt they try to escape.

Their sudden directness is sometimes disconcerting if one is not prepared for it, and a remark made can sometimes hit too closely to the truth for comfort. They know how to assert themselves when necessary, and can be completely oblivious to the effect they have on others. Unless other factors in the chart indicate it, they do not intend to intentionally challenge anyone, but their way of stating something can somehow bring others up short.

Aspects from Jupiter
Lilith magnifies whatever degree of extroversion and independence exists. The spirit of adventure is strong, with an unusual affinity for nature. There is a fierce independence, a roaming spirit, that underlies the outer makeup. It accounts for a bachelor-like attitude, even when married, that leads to fewer personal ties. They will rarely admit it as such, and actually minimize it lest it be misunderstood. There is an uneasy suspicion of anyone they feel may be interested in

them personally, because of the possibility that relationship demands would interfere with the freedom to come and go as they please. They see it as a potential future barrier to their independence. At first they shy away or literally buck at being tamed, which is the way they see serious relationships, using any lifestyle excuse from perennial college attendance to professional dedication to advertising themselves as poor relationship risks. However, they are attracted to those with strong qualities of independence or those who travel in their work, which more or less guarantees their own freedom to come and go. In this case they make solid mates who love to share the partner's adventure. This is not to say they can always live with the kind of independence or free-roaming spirit expressed by the partner, because what they want is a definite commitment that does not interfere in their own freer lifestyle.

Lilith magnifies their need for broadening their horizons or for the "thrill of the hunt." Thus, even when not involved in exploring new pathways (mentally or physically) during more stationary periods, they nonetheless hold on to this option with an attitude of "don't fence me in." This can result in sudden separations from time to time, either affectionally, through their work, or for another reason. Among people with Lilith-Jupiter aspects we have many writers of books, people in the broadcasting field, and university teachers. The artists among them always manage to bring in the feeling of movement in their work. For those in politics, interest lies more in national government rather than the local level.

Generosity and support for others' expansion and growth is strong, even encouraged, but is given rather paternally. In other words, it is given more or less in line with what they feel is right for the other person. This is not to say it is given selfishly; it is simply what they enjoy doing.

They are not undependable in relationships in the classical sense of the word, but see too much dependency on them as a trap. They cannot abide being dependent themselves, and for this reason will never relate entirely to the responsibility here—the bachelor-like attitude. Instead, they will pursue their own interests more avidly, figuring others will get over it, still remain devoted, and grateful for their being or having been with you. They are not as much conceited as they are of a very high opinion of themselves. These people are difficult to dislike because of their magnanimous spirit, directness, and basic good humor. In all the aspects, there is something different about their overall philosophy of life or their basic lifestyle. It may be because of wealth or simply looking at life from a wealthier perspective.

No matter how conservative the chart is otherwise, these people relish an occasional gamble as if to test their luck, which is a strong consideration because of their instinctive feeling that God is in His heaven and all is right with the world. They simply wish to make sure Jupiter aspects from Lilith prompt a strong universality or God consciousness through which, on its higher level, one may effectively inspire others to greater faith through their preoccupation with searching the pathways of life or religion. In trine it it could indicate well balanced beliefs grounded in faith (Meher Baba). On its lower level or harshly asepcted, it could be the religious zealot who attracts people to his or her teachings, urging their dependence on his or her interpretations, and then preying on their weakness for self-aggrandizement, particularly if Jupiter is harshly aspected to Saturn and conjunct Pluto (Rev. Jim Jones). Both examples are, of course, the extreme, which are naturally different in effect according to each individual chart.

Lilith aspects from Jupiter magnify support for any interests that circumvent the personal ego. These aspects bring periods of opportunity for sudden successful growth, approval, and appreciation when activated. However, when selfishly motivated, they also serve to support its negative trend toward overextending themselves in something that will cost them dearly or continually deny any satisfaction from it. Inharmonious aspects from Jupiter may mark periods when things are made too easy, giving the native an easy way out of something that later proves very costly. There is temptation to take advantage, falsely promote something for selfish gain, or in some way to bend the letter of the law. They may attract such persons.

The conjunction may remove just enough challenge to overcome difficulties, so that they waste many years leading a superficial existence. In this case too much of a good thing may create wasted years if the emphasis is on ease rather than on the means it gives them to grow in knowledge. If they involve themselves in something creatively meaningful, according to their higher interests, there is opportunity par excellance.

Aspects from Saturn
Lilith conjunct or in close aspect to Saturn indicates people who take nothing for granted. They are not natural skeptics as much as they are they are people who have to learn to incorporate skepticism into their nature. This is not necessarily bad, but simply stems from their need to heighten their awareness to facts as they are, minus any rationalization. Through experience they learn not to move on anything before considering its useful merits or to cooperate with those things they fear are ineffective. This and a certain suspicion of things is healthy enough and leads to better judgment. However, when personalities get involved, or in areas that do not circumvent the personal ego, organized clarity is denied, particularly if Lilith is in a fire sign. In this instance, they can become incredibly pessimistic, troubled, or deeply worrisome, many times overdramatizing the projected pitfalls because of the emotional static they cannot or refuse to rise above. This is seen by others as a strange character twist in one who is usually seen as a well-organized individual.

Lilith in a water sign aspected to Saturn in an earth sign appears to particularly sharpen the defenses on personal and emotional levels to a sometimes aggressive, but always authoritarian, response to those whom they fear are inept, useless, or a security threat. If both Lilith and Saturn are in water signs, the pessimism may be turned on themselves, leading to a dangerously unhealthy state of mind (Marilyn Monroe).

If Lilith is in an air sign (Gemini, Libra, Aquarius), aspects from Saturn assist in conceptual direction. The formation of mental impressions are arrived at through greater mental organization, investigation, and formalization. As writers, the work is laboriously done to the smallest detail and is well organized. So much so that unless they can remain successfully depersonalized in their work and forget about their critics, they can attempt such total organization as to run the risk of making things sterile if they do not feel hopelessly defeated before they start. In the softer aspects or with sufficient impersonality, they still work as conscientiously, but without the risk of sterility because of a clearer perspective and knowing enough to get away from things every so often. This is particularly true if Neptune is strong enough in the chart to keep them from losing the inspiration that keeps it from being deadened by detail, belaboring points or driving them into the ground.

When negative there are severe authority problems. But, positive or negative, no matter the cut of the chart otherwise, in all these people you can sense an inner brooding or an attitude of preparedness should the sky start to fall. Here, security (in the personal sense) is never successfully minimized, and they will work hard and put up with a great deal for it. They often attract those who are successful in what they do and are hard workers, admiring what they relate to or seek more of in themselves.

Pure pleasure for the sake of it is not something they can ever be totally at ease with unless in some way it serves a utilitarian or political purpose, even if it is only their own. At its best this combination eventually brings home to them that we are our brother's keeper, in that if a project fails they are in some way responsible if they do not incorporate some form or system or speak up about what they know works or is right. The combination nags at their awareness of responsibility for others, and for personal achievement. Whether they choose to respond to this consistent urging or simply to find fault in others who do not depends on the rest of the chart.

Under positive aspect or attitudes, these people can be incredibly self-disciplined and forebearing, or under negative aspects or attitudes, exacting and rigid. The highest wisdom one can attain from Lilith aspects to Saturn is in the understanding of and acceptance of the words, "Whom the Lord loveth, He chasteneth."

Aspects from Uranus
Aspects from Uranus explain the unpredictability or separativeness in personal affairs. They must be free souls. While gracious in friendship, they nevertheless keep peculiarly detached unless they can offer purposeful or helpful assistance. But they prefer to get away from others if too much attention is focused on them because this threatens possible interference with separativeness they reserve for themselves. They instinctively shun overinvolvement in the passing scene, which is just how they see it: a passing scene that they merely pass through.

Orientation to the future is very strong. When the future finally becomes a part of the contemporary scene, it is dealt with in the same way—as utilitarian to another future. They tread lightly in the present, maintaining an emotional distance as if to avoid stagnation and losing sight of tomorrow. There is no rudeness intended. Lilith merely acts as a magnifying glass to Uranus, haunting, teasing, and tempting them with certainty of greater happiness in a future to come. The fascination is to the future and to any hedge against crystallization in the status quo, to which they can never completely relate.

They see things from the viewpoint of temporary utility, and the status quo as a means to an end but not as an end in itself. If some thing or situation lacks a useful purpose, they would rather it not take up unnecessary time or space. They are more concerned with progressive ideas and people who are progressive than with concrete objects, crystallized situations, or contemporary ideas. Whether they admit this depends on the amount of passiveness shown in the chart. Nevertheless they all feel anxiety about any overinvolvement unless it serves a future purpose or is progressive. Basically liberal in their viewpoint, they inwardly abhor, and in one way or another separate themselves from petty events or ideas.

They believe people should be able to do as they please with minimum supervision. Believing in complete freedom of thought and action, they can nonetheless maintain amazingly rigid disciplines when and for however long it is necessary. This is because they acknowledge a natural justice: every action carries its own future reward or punishment. However, in personal derelictions of duty, they do not see that the punishment should be all that serious, while the future rewards for helpful actions should be substantial.

They will work hard, not taking too seriously (personally) the frustrations of any daily irritations as long as they can look forward to future happiness. They are the ones most apt to say, "Grow old with me for the best is yet to come." Such a future orientation keeps a certain youth about them that is active far into old age as a result of the expectancy and the hope about what is yet to come. They enjoy surprises, as if they represent a burst of fresh air from the present.

They can be exasperating at times in that while seemingly content to be caught up for a time in petty matters, other factors in the chart being equal, they may do a complete about face that seems to make no sense at all to those around them. It may very well not make any sense to them either except to finally relieve the growing sense of stagnation that suddenly becomes unbearably stifling. The relief it gives to them, from a situation they fear is cutting off their air, is enough for them to feel free again for something else, anything else, so long as there is some more useful purpose in it. Lilith's seductive signal to something distant when aspecting Uranus is enough to continually lure them onward. Action is always more or less sudden when it follows a too long stagnant (for them) situation, creating little earthquakes in relationships from time to time.

When involved in something progressive, scientific, or humanely utilitarian, they are extremely steady, dedicated, and incredibly loyal workers, as if nourished by the rewards of the future it promises and content to be a part of it. When positive, they can be the most inventive of people; have fine talent for writing; and interest in air travel, astrology, technology, missiles and rocketry (Werner Von Braun), the unusual (Robert Ripley), or the bizarre in artistic expression (Federico Fellini).

When negative, you may still see the human interest, but more personally biased, as in Anita Bryant, who made her battle against homosexual rights for the good of the human condition a distorted crusade. Although sextile Uranus, the blend of the opposition of Neptune to Lilith in her eighth house blinded her vision to carry what she considered her humanitarian crusade to dangerous proportions of intolerance. When positive, the concern for the human condition gave us such people as Carl Jung, Martin Luther King, Jr., and Helen Keller.

Aspects from Neptune
These people seem to automatically sense the dangers inherent in the psychic forces around them. For a time, until they can handle, understand, or come to terms with their sensitivity, they will deny it—even totally if Saturn is harshly aspected to Neptune. This is from some strange fear they cannot necessarily explain but can definitely sense. They are sensitive, unusually ildealistic, and somewhat gullible. But it seems they have only to be taken advantage of once for them to react with more suspicion the next time. If Neptune is in a positive sign, and given enough time, they may more realistically adjust to disillusionment than if it were in a negative sign. In the latter case the reaction is all the more emotional and thus more difficult to come to terms with, affecting an important relationship or the health, depending on the house Neptune rules.

There may be artistic or musical talent, or an early exposure to culture that enriches their background. It adds a quiet gentleness to the character or the tendency to slip away from an area in which they are uncomfortable. It softens the nature and describes one who is reclusive from time to time. They are psychic, but deny it to all but a selective few. There is a great preoccupation with love and ideals. They will put the sincerity of that above all other considerations in a relationship. It is as if to be sincere is to be automatically forgiven. When the aspect is activated by progression, transit, or eclipse, the gullibility or sensitivity is severely tested because it is at these times that they see things through incredibly rose-colored glasses.

It is also at these times that they can grow spiritually through culture, prayer, meditation, or selflessness if they are accepting the reality of a foolish ideal from which Lilith, magnifying Neptune, is nagging an awakening. There may be opportunity to help or act as a sounding board to someone who is in some way handicapped socially, physically, financially, or through attitude. Ordinarily, they are far too sensitive, if not incredibly naive for their surroundings, until they

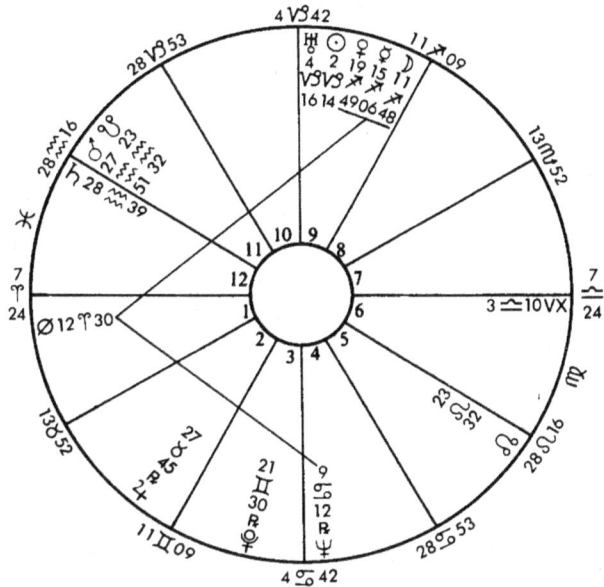

Chart 13. Howard Hughes, December 24, 1905, 12:33 p.m., Houston Texas; source4: Lloyd Cope

become more pragmatic in their approach to life. Many times they hide their heads in the sand rather than see what they do not wish to see, as if pretending it isn't there will make it so. Pollyanna must have had this aspect in spades.

Lilith in aspect to Neptune exaggerates whatever the degree of receptivity in the makeup, creating an unusually strong inner life and one that is particularly out of proportion with reality when self-centered. When selfishly intended, innocent or not, or if the emotions are misdirected or undisciplined, Lilith denies a successful outlet to Neptune's higher level of inner guidance or the magnified creative imagination. This is because it distorts and confuses the emotional nature, and is therefore debilitating. Lilith is alien to the personal desires, and these people are apt to keep these desires on a pedestal and literally blind themselves to whatever or whoever may deny them. When there is no emotional objectivity to make them independent of emotional fears or biases, the Lilith energy buildup literally turns in on itself to completely veil the person from certain facts. This causes serious self-defeating errors in judgment. Particularly when negative, Lilith magnifies illusion to unhealthy levels. Thus, in sensitizing the person's Neptune ray to unusually deep wells of etheric energy, Lilith to Neptune aspects account for the extraordinarily creative imagination when positive (either by attitude or aspect), and illusion or self-delusion when negative (either by attitude or by aspect).

An extreme example of the negative imagination is Howard Hughes, who had Lilith square Neptune and both angular. It manifested through his incredible hypochondria, ruled by Neptune. He demanded sterilization of everything that came near him during his years of retirement. His total self-centeredness at that time (Lilith in Aries) and the childish fears (Lilith's lower fear, or in his case, neurotic level) in his personal makeup were blatantly displayed through his magnified germ consciousness and self-protective seclusion against an unclean world. Nevertheless, at the other extreme, the creative level of his imagination was a near genius in the movie and airplane industries.

In conjunction, this is the classical sensitive: the natural musician, dancer, artist, or psychologist. These people knows there is more to life than meets the eye. The degree of impersonality, as well as aspects, will determine whether they are helped by others in their ability to handle their talents or sensitivity and whether they will accept it, or be left to flounder in personal chaos because of selfish emphasis on his dream or an illusion.

Although the powerful awareness of nether worlds may create a self-undoing sensitivity, personal naivete, or gullibility, when or where they can forget about themselves it brings out a charisma so powerful that people treat them as totally special, as if larger than life. It is strange but true. Remember that Lilith is extreme either way. Interest in the psychology of people, or what used to be called people-wisdom, comes naturally to them. Whether they use it or abuse it depends on their ability to depersonalize, particularly in the matters or with the people of the house ruled by Neptune and Lilith.

Aspects from Pluto
When impersonally involved, these people can be very pursuasive. They know just what to say (or not to say) at the right time for the strongest effect; otherwise, they are just as apt to keep silent rather than expose how they feel. They have unusually strong powers of observation and almost all of them, barring other factors in the chart, have some degree of extra sensory perception. They are good in work of a secret nature.

No one is likely to ever know all there is to know about them, no matter the appearance given to the contrary. They instinctively know the value of a certain amount of privacy but are not necessarily obvious about it. They prefer, instead, that others remain unaware of this important personal need in order to avoid any undue curiosity, which makes them distinctly uneasy about interference. They are (or become) quite expert at drawing attention away from their vulnerable areas and their private ideas until they feel in control of the situation. They prefer to be more active in the background until then. They are a force to eventually be reckoned with if they feel exposed to personal attack, criticism, or denial. But within areas that avoid personality involvements they welcome criticism as a challenge, and if you are correct they will admire you for it.

Pride is usually strong. However, it is not usually a problem unless others come too close to something personal they wish to avoid having attention focused on and prefer to deal with strictly by themselves. In this case they may appear to be open enough about it, instinctively realizing that obvious secrecy would only stir curiosity and risk interference. However, if another's curiosity is too great, there is a growing adamance because of what they see as a possible invasion of their privacy. Their forcefulness becomes apparent (usually through attitude), but always in a subtle way that suddenly puts others in a strangely defensive position, as if their integrity is on the line. This soon conveys the message that they prefer to be left alone; it is as though the other person came too close to territory they have claimed as their own, and the door is closed to in a way that leaves others with a distinct feeling of having been somehow overpowered. The gracious outer demeanor suddenly seems to be warning others away. Others may emotionally pick up on their resentment of the "intrusion" and find themselves left with a strange feeling of upset and having been somehow punished or turned on without knowing why or what really happened. When necessary they can be downright sarcastic, putting you on the defensive as if an apology were in order but you do not know why.

People with Lilith aspecting Pluto are unusually vulnerable. At some time in life they may have been too predictable or obvious, exposing themselves to forces or persons they felt undermined the control of their own affairs. Once extricated from this they realize only too well their vulnerability and go to great lengths to avoid (or do away with) any unnecessary personal spotlights on themselves. In fact, public figures will do what they can to underplay the prestigious trappings of their position and themselves, but never their power (Jimmy Carter). They like to keep a certain personal invisibility, not so much about their outer or professional life as in their personal involvement behind it. However, when blinded by personality involvement, they have been known to state something penetrating about themselves that once and for all does away with curiosity about a particular area from which they fear attack (reasonable or not). Mr. Carter did this when he spoke of his "lust" during an interview for *Playboy*.

There is either an interest in the paranormal or they are in contact with persons of such interest. There may be an awakening of unusual powers, as in the case of Uri Geller, famous Russian psychic, known particularly for his work in psychokinesis. Mr. Geller has Lilith in Scorpio in the first house square a conjunction of Pluto-Saturn in the tenth. Lilith magnified to incredible heights the psychic potential of a Scorpio stellium in his first house square the tenth house conjunction.

People with Lilith-Pluto aspects know how to relate to those in positions of power or potential power and many times develop strong friendships. They influence projects from behind the scenes and make invaluable advisers if they believe in what is being done. There is nothing lukewarm about these people. They are either for something or it is non-existent. They have unusual attunement to mass psychology, which Jim Jones (Lilith conjunct Saturn opposition Pluto) took to the negative extreme in Jonestown, Guyana, with mass suicide-murder in 1978. In literature is Alex Haley (Lilith trine Pluto), author of *Roots*, a work that triggered a sense of pride in black people for their historical background, which was no small feat at the time.

Crusading tendencies are strong in people with Lilith-Pluto connections. Whether the motivation is positive or negative is what makes the difference for good or evil. With the hard aspects, selfish temptations are by far stronger; but if the dedication to the Lord's work surpasses desire for personal power, Lilith aligned to Pluto can be a sure guide for working miracles.

Lilith's Solstice Point

A planet's solstice point is simply its distance from its nearest solstice carried over to the other side of that solstice. It is a relatively easy point to find. Simply determine the degrees and minutes remaining for Lilith in the sign that it is in in order to obtain the degrees and minutes of its solstice point. The sign to use is given in the table below.

Aries	*Virgo*	*Libra*	*Pisces*
Virgo	Aries	Pisces	Libra
Taurus	Leo	Scorpio	Aquarius
Leo	Taurus	Aquarius	Scorpio
Gemini	Cancer	Capricorn	Sagittarius
Cancer	Gemini	Sagittarius	Capricorn

Example: If natal Lilith is in 26 Gemini 18, then 3°42′ remain in Gemini. Cancer is the solstice sign for Gemini, so the solstice point for Lilith is 3 Cancer 42.

The solstice point of Lilith when activated by a heavy transit, solar eclipse, or progression, marks a turning point that will affect the individual's vocation or reputation in the future. Rather than marking an event, it appears to mark the beginning stage of something that may reach various stages of development each time natal Lilith is strongly activated. It may mark an event, but the event is not as much a significator of something brought to a head as much as it is an indication of a turn in the road that is necessary for future direction. If missed, it is the source of future troublespots due to lack of growth; in other words, the point at which things can begin to sour if the individual ignores the surrounding tides of change within or without.

For example, transiting Saturn conjunct the Lilith solstice point can mark a productive turning point. Much depends upon whether the indivdiual is willing to accept a long-term commitment, or a particular responsibility, as necessary for some future achievement. Otherwise, it can mark the beginning of an ending situation that dates back to this time. A Jupiter transit conjunct Lilith (particularly if by retrograde motion, Jupiter makes several crossings) may mark the period when greater education should be seriously considered or activities extended over a broader base.

Direct the solstice point by one degree a year and note any planets it aspects. Look particularly for aspects to the ruler of the tenth house, Saturn, and planets in the tenth for vocational insights.

Directions

By direction at 3° per year (approximate mean motion of 3°), Lilith will square itself in between the ages of 29 and 30, more or less during the period of the Saturn return. This accounts for the dual turning points in maturation that one experiences at this time: first in emotional perspective for self-sustainment (Lilith), and secondly for material coping and the adult structuring of life (Saturn). Lilith will oppose itself between the ages of 59 and 60, about the time of the second Saturn return, to polarize (with Saturn) the consciousness toward final fulfillment of one's adult obligations and the stern realization of what has been accomplished in the major years of adulthood.

These are both significant periods of realization—the first being the crystallizing adulthood of the self with all that it implies, and the second being the results of that adulthood in the collective sphere. The dual influence of Saturn by transit and Lilith by direction at these crucial focal points of responsibility and realization in life, and the depersonalizing effects they both have, is not without significance in studying the nature of Lilith. Both Saturn and Lilith mark the crucial but necessary maturing processes working simultaneously, indicating the natural affinity of which Sepharial spoke—Saturn on the physical/material level and Lilith on the emotional one. Both levels of the individual are stressed for natural conclusions at these times, the first to conclude the youthful years, and the second to conclude the most dynamically productive ones.

Consider further the period of the first opposition of Saturn to itself between the ages of 14 and 15 approximately. By direction Lilith is at this time in semisquare to itself natally. This is the first significant period, when teenagers face the traditional and emotional (Saturn and Lilith) disciplines placed on them as a result of their developing sexual powers. This is an emotional friction between what they have known before and their budding awareness of the world of affection between the sexes, and a necessary part of their emotional maturation for the responsibility such power carries for the future.

The urges of whatever planet Lilith aspects by direction are highly magnified (or distorted). This lasts about one year, and it makes people susceptible to strange influences, or at least those strange to the individual, or compulsive actions related to the matters ruled by the planet or house. If the house is on the western side of the chart, it may be a reaction to the actions of others.

Aspecting Mercury by direction, Lilith sharpens the imagination to a fine edge; but communication is subject to distortion if these people cannot rise above personal ego or emotional static. A compulsion for study, travel, and new ideas is noticeable. They become easily bored by the mundane and avoid uninteresting people. This direction of Lilith may also account for a year of unusual preoccupation with health and fitness, diet, or strange culinary appetites because Mercury naturally rules the sixth sign. If Mercury rules the natal fifth house, children are a frustration and there are problems if honest lines of communication have never been developed. But the overall effect is to become acutely aware of children as nothing more than small adults and to treat them accordingly. They may have to deal with a young person who is different or has done something socially unacceptable by ordinary social standards. For the naturally creative individual, talent, whatever it may be, is incredibly heightened. This year may well be one for great creative growth or productivity. This influence also heightens literary talent.

Aspecting the Sun by direction, willfulness and a biting need to do their own thing creates quite a change in the character or life. These people will carefully cut themselves off from those who overshadow their individuality, usually doing so without explanation. Leadership urges grow strong during this year and account for firing an ambition they have never before known. Resentment of comparisons made between themselves and others are carefully held in check, but pushed too far, they can become surprisingly egotistical or scorching in attitude. Undoubtedly, they have a special talent in something, no matter how large or small, that could be appreciated now if they will concentrate on the talent or interest rather than themselves.

Whichever planet is being aspected by Lilith by direction, the basic urges it represents (Venus, social; Saturn, duty; Moon, domestic; and so on) must be depersonalized. Unless these matters are approached more logically, unselfishly, or creatively for the greater good, losses, upsets, and denials can plague these things this year.

Dignity
Because of Lilith's affinity with Saturn, Lilith's support of Saturn realizations by direction during the most crucial period of maturation in the individual (Saturn return), and iits depersonalizing effects to prepare the native for the adult future, Lilith is obviously dignified in Capricorn, home of Saturn. It is in this impersonal executive sign, and the one most alien to emotional static, that Lilith's qualities of impersonality and depersonalization can most readily identify. Consider Lilith as the co-ruler of Capricorn, and when studying the condition of the house with Capricorn on the cusp, look also to Lilith's placement by sign, house, and aspect in the natal chart in order to gain a clearer picture of the conditions.

Lilith's is in detriment in Cancer, home of the Moon and Lilith's natural antithesis. In Cancer, Lilith magnifies the emotions too greatly for easy experiences of depersonalization in this sign of sentiment, family, and emotional dependencies. Those with Lilith in this sign must carefully design a life around the emotional comforts of others in order to maintain their personal composure and accomplish what they want to do. In this sign Lilith creates the constant need for personal evaluation and the development of a protective coating of graciousness in order to avoid the exaggerated emotional reactions to the moods of others. Lilith in Cancer can be successfully dealt with if the individual will channel the lunar tendencies through an occupation that is either ruled by the Moon or takes in one of its rulerships. It is good for public dealings, particularly in the literary or arts world, or for a specialized product, or one that is out of the ordinary.

Chapter 6

Lilith in Return Charts

The house that Lilith motivates—in other words, Lilith's house position in a return chart—continually appears to be a significant area that contributes the special coloring or whatever uniqueness there may be to the period. By house, Lilith will indicate the particular area, person, or thing that preoccupies your mind during that year or month, aside from whatever else may be going on. You may ignore it or not, depending on whatever else is happening in your life. It may be a preoccupation because of something different that you had not before realized, a nagging awareness that somehow things may not be the same, a surprising development that brings something to your attention, something that has become very special, or a distortion you just cannot understand. The distortion may be in yourself.

Just as in the natal chart, Lilith in return charts denies satisfaction or distorts things on personal levels (emotionally), but is characteristically rewarding or beautifully inspiring when you live in the higher nature. A person associated with the house (for example, the ninth of inlaws) is apt to do something different. This is true unless activity associated with this house is already out of the ordinary, of an intellectual or creative nature, or there is unselfish intent. In this case, things run extraordinarily well or great inspiration is felt. It may be a unique experience.

Aspects are important of course, but basically where naive or self-centered attitudes prevail (no matter how innocent or self-justified the reason), you experience denial of one sort of another or feel intimidated by someone. Particularly within ordinary daily exchanges, you may encounter a coldness from someone who seems ridiculous to the situation, or have to deal with someone who makes you distinctly uncomfortable. In reality, it is sparked by feelings of an unreasonable inferiority in the other person that take you by surprise or keep you in an anxious state. At the opposite extreme, where unselfish or impersonal attitudes prevail, things go unusually well. It is only under circumstances that bypass emotional static that the mind and imagination are greatly sharpened and confidence is heightened.

This house matter may not necessarily dominate a period because, of course, this depends on other factors. Nevertheless, one of Lilith's house matters appears to hold your special attention, interest, fascination, or urgency, or it simply keeps your mind preoccupied as if something about it is missing. You've either lost interest or control in these matters, or activity and expected satisfaction is denied.

Lilith in the First House
When Lilith is in the first house, for example, you may be continually occupied with yourself, your health, or your appearance now. You may feel less confident than usual and need proof of being appreciated along with a secret desire to be singled out, favored, or somehow recognized. Of course the more you seek such reassurance which you may think you're automatically entitled to, the more it will be denied. Others feel intimidated by some sort of coldness from you, possibly from the self-preoccupation to which they cannot relate. They see that something is unusual or different about you now, but they do not know what. Your self-preoccupation unwittingly makes you seem distant. Lilith can create just this type of vicious circle unless you do a 180° turn and just forget about yourself. The more you can do this (or are naturally detached), and identify yourself through what you do and your ideals rather than whether you are being appreciated, the more confident you will feel, not to mention being fascinating to others. The detachment releases the self-preoccupation that makes you seem distant, and the apparent sophistication makes you particularly interesting.

The interest of others in you now, while denied or meaningless on personality levels where there is naturally more emotional static, becomes respect and admiration on creative, intellectual, or otherwise impersonal levels. Projecting yourself through ideas rather than personalities, or what you do rather than what you are, is the key to a personality maturation period indicated by the return as being necessary.

Depersonalization is essential in order to rise above the usual or any limited views you have, as well as petty or selfish desires. They will only trigger denials or distortions because of a blindspot. Keep in mind Lilith's affinity with Saturn, which while denying personal gratification, will reward accomplishment and socially creative intent.

In the solar return, the sign that Lilith tenants indicates the particular characteristics and/or interests that are being magnified in you this year, either noticeably or by their absence. In the lunar return, however, Lilith's sign indicates through what rulership it is carried out or, if living in the lower nature, where it is denied or distorted. For example, Lilith in Libra, during the solar return year, would focus a seemingly aggressive curiosity through diplomatic (and at times not so diplomatic) questioning. The drive to create balance at any cost becomes almost a complusion wherever serious imbalance is suspected. The impersonality with which the individual moves to equalize things, good or bad, and the preference to go it alone if full independence is denied, more or less colors the year. If Lilith is in Sagittarius in the lunar return, for example, this may be done where an in-law, someone at a distance, or a legal principle in a court battle is concerned.

In one case with Lilith in Virgo in a solar return, sensitivity to detail of techniques was magnified, creating greater than usual anxiety about things being done as conscientiously and perfectly as possible. More attention than usual was paid to health, fitness, and practical safety measures. In one of the lunar returns for that year she had Lilith in Cancer in the ninth house. In that month Lilith was noticeable through a family situation (Cancer), in this case a grandson (ninth) who was visiting for a month. She gave time and energy every day to teach him proper swimming techniques so that he would be safe in the water, and also to build him up physically.

Always give particular attention to the house that Lilith is applying to, as it appears to have the greater influence than does the one it is leaving, where it seems to show weaker significance except during the early part of the period. You might say that the interest of the house Lilith is in is for a purpose related to the house it is in applying to.

For example, in the ninth house applying to the tenth, you may be preoccupied with people or matters at or from a distance that need attention in order to clear the way for something to do with your vocation, reputation, or a partner. Also note that there is an emphasized effect for an event if Lilith is occupying the same house or sign in a return that it occupies natally.

Note the sign that Lilith is in during the period for greater insight into Lilith's effect in the house it occupies. For instance, Lilith in Scorpio in the tenth house of the return may introduce a nagging persistence for checking into job affiliated insurance benefits, pensions, or the like. There may be a power struggle that involves the future conditions or management under which you must work. If Lilith is in Sagittarius in the sixth house, there may be a important work you must submit to a national office. In Sagittarius, it focuses matters at a distance, risks, or expansions that affect your work, or people from a distance who appreciate its merit. Lilith in Libra in the seventh would create a double emphasis on partnership or a legal matter. There may be unusual changes taking place in the affairs with or of the mate, or something done that changes his or her appearance. The partner seems more remote, removed from the usual daily matters, and more easily intimidated.

If a natal aspect or the sign position of Lilith is being repeated in the return chart the period is highly significant because this natural characteristic is surfacing for outer expression (an event). In one lunar return chart, Lilith at 24 Gemini 32 in the seventh was trine the Libra Moon conjunct Venus, ruler of the fifth. Natal Lilith at 26 Gemini 18 was trine the Moon but square Venus in the fifth. It was in this month that the husband had an important business trip that made him feel anxious because of certain persons he would meet there. Instead, he abruptly decided to take a trip in the other direction, cross country, to be reunited with their daughter whom he had not seen for many years. The change in his travel plans came as a complete surprise, and he was on his way the following afternoon. The woman preferred not to go, preferring the time alone; but she was pleased for the chance her husband and daughter would have to become close again. This aspect of Lilith trine the Moon in her natal chart had always surfaced as a certain independence in that she preferred to stay away from family gatherings; this time was no exception.

In the Second House
In the second house you may find yourself more than usually preoccupied with possessions, security, or getting better value for your money, although you will probably avoid giving this impression to everyone except those close to you. There may be preoccupation with shopping, particularly for items that signify the different values and personal tastes you have been developing and want to indulge. You quietly enjoy obtaining even the smallest items that say something about you that is different; you may haunt strange places that offer the unusual; you may enjoy unusual or exotic foods. There is less appetite for the ordinary or usual. Things considered in fashion leave you cold. Rather, you desire to express the idea of yourself in what you choose, have, or surround yourself with—the spirit of yourself through which you may value genuine little items that came from a foreign port for which you have always felt a strange *deja vu*. There is pleasing satisfaction in owning and touching these things. If you are traveling this month you relish finding little shops that have such items, or dealing with such merchants.

With secret relish you may enjoy disposing of things you have disliked for a long time and replacing them with something that is more you, even enjoying the breaking of it as you throw it away as if in defiance of what it stood for. At the very least the urge is strong to rid yourself of things that no longer express you taste. Particularly if Lilith is in Scorpio, you see it as junk and are willing to give it away no matter the monetary value.

In keeping with Lilith's affinity to Saturn, it is a rewarding time to look for especially low cost, old, or used items that now are unusual. Haunt garage or estate sales, check flea markets, or obtain hand-me-downs that satisfy a kink in your personality. Your mind may be preoccupied with a large future purchase you realize you plan to make.

Where music is concerned (the higher second house rulership), your taste runs to the unusual. You may hear fascinating music that you have never heard before. If Lilith is negative, the noise factor around you may be high in this period, or you may hear some of the worst music you have ever heard.

Where ordinary things are concerned you could be quite miserly if not downright covetous, although you would be the last to admit it. Nevertheless, you are a bit surprised about this in yourself when the return is over. During the return you tend to run to extremes where money is concerned, one time giving generously and at another secretly resenting any suspected selfishness for your money, as if two sides of your nature were at war with each other. Even generosity at this time is carried in your mind as something the other person should be eternally grateful for. It is during this period that you may have become aware of another's use of money that involves your own and that you disapprove of, and may secretly vow to make less available from now on.

Your values system may be severely tested at this time. A bargain may present itself that ordinarily might not interest you, but now fascinates you into parting with money you can ill afford to spend. If your basic sense of values leaves a lot to be desired, feelings of being poor may plague you now. If this is so, the awareness that you are poor is in the higher values that you do not recognize. Beware of someone selling something at a steal. It may be just that—stolen property. Lilith is calling for mental, esthetic, and spiritual values to rise in you now. Do not misinterpret this and be misguided into material greed in order to fill a void you feel.

In the Third House
During this return period you may find your mind able to roam back with unusual clarity over every delicious detail to any experience you wish to recall. Through such mental wanderings it is as if you were watching it all happen again, but now through the mind's eye where you can sharply evaluate them as you roll it backward and forward at will.

Depending on the chart, communications may be garbled; in other words, misunderstood from what you intended. Realizing this, and particularly if Scorpio or Pluto are rising or are strong, you may choose not to accept phone calls. Indeed, you may take the phone off the hook and not be at home to certain visitors, creating a communication blackout of sorts for yourself. In this case there is an abhorrent or secret fear of receiving a visit from one or more people whom you wish to avoid. Remember that Lilith exaggerates, thus creating these observed overreactions. What might simply be a nuisance at another time takes on major proportions under Lilith.

There might be an unusual circumstance with a neighbor, or you might receive a surprise visit from a former one you never expected to see again. Affairs of a sibling may come to light during this time.

Intuition may be sharply heightened. There may be prophetic feelings about something you will do in the future. You may find yourself preparing for it but not knowing when or why.

For teachers, the ability to function with students is frustrated if personalities become involved, or the desire to not even bother. Otherwise, such matters go unusually well at this time. It is the atmosphere of impersonality that makes the difference.

For writers there may be acute awareness of the need for some improvement in their style. It can be a rewarding time for clarity and self-criticism, and a time when past constructive criticism of your work can begin being applied. It is a particularly rewarding time to research information or receive important information from another. Past work worthy of praise may suddenly be recognized. Mental types gain much from this position of Lilith. There may be travel.

When living in the lower nature, feelings of intellectual inferiority, feeling stupid, or being afraid of conversation may suddenly break forward into the consciousness. Lilith is simply focusing the realization about how much you do not know and how much more you need to know. Lilith in the third house of the return can act as one of those important turning points that stimulates you to greater study, then or at a later date. Or it may at least signal your lack in some area of study, which you will now or later realize is your weak spot. Lilith appears to work as a mode of transmission for the awakening vibrations of Uranus, the higher octave of the mind, in this case exposing your mental famine to your secret self.

In the Fourth House
Lilith in the fourth house of a return chart often marks a time during which you will travel and be a house guest, stay at a hotel, go camping, or somehow be removed from home or immediate family affairs. It may be a time of hospitalization, or one at a place that is other than the usual; in other words, sleeping elsewhere. This may also be the case when the return Lilith is in Cancer or heavily aspecting the ruler of the fourth house or a planet in that house. In those cases where the person is not away from home for a time, he or she may stay up far into the night for whatever reason, thus staying out of the bedroom.

In the fourth Lilith is simply creating a sense of displacement within the usual domestic routine, or a displacement from it entirely for a time. You will usually be more relaxed during the period away from the routine, but when at home you are more than usually concerned that it be orderly in order to be able to function there. This is your way of ensuring calm waters and getting precious time for yourself for other things that compel your interest now. If anything, your domestic efficiency might rise, or at least you'll have more congenial relations with others in your home. Order can make for the emotional comfort of others and this is important to you now. It is not as much for their comfort as it is for your own, in order to ensure being personally unaffected by them. It may appear very smooth but if graciously done is actually rather deliberate. This is done to keep everyone content lest something go wrong and you are interfered with or misunderstood by the family, because you desire now to be independent of them. Otherwise, anxiety sparks sudden resentful reactions and trouble that is blown out of proportion.

Staying up late into the night satisfies, if only in left-handed way, the desire to be free of those in the home or its daily atmosphere for a while and to do something different. Then again, you may satisfy the desire to roam with a getaway. A trip that did not appeal to you before may preoccupy your mind now; you may be oblivious to the reason, and only aware that you would like to be elsewhere.

When positive, Lilith liberates. This may be a time when you finally attract some help that in one way or another frees your time. This is a good time for personal hobbies or creative projects in the home. You feel more removed from daily affairs and prefer now to indulge your own.

In the Fifth House
When in the fifth house of entertainment, you may find yourself on a radio or television show, or in the unique position of sponsoring or being a guest speaker. Consider this also if Lilith is aspecting the fifth house ruler.

For mental or artistic types this position of Lilith is a boon to creative expression, bringing flashes of inspiration and heightened creative confidence, and/or attracting someone who believes in and encourages your talent. On the negative side, or when living in your lower nature, you may be nagged by feelings of being unfairly stripped of your individuality, being treated as just another face in the crowd and resenting it. Or inwardly you bemoan a talent you never did anything or enough with. You may see special talent in one of your children or a young person now that you could easily encourage or inspire. For yourself, remember, that it is never too late.

Heed Lilith's hauntings that preoccupy your thoughts to sharpen a talent. Take that class or be creative in any way that you feel a desire for—from practicing on the piano to cooking or sewing to submitting an article to a magazine. Study yoga, paint, make music, photograph, or do something else. If you are talented in crafts, you may be surprised at the good work you can do now. If you are a dancer, writer, musician, or occultist by profession, your work is inspired. Let the creative juices flow. However, if you get caught up in personalities or your own importance, you will flounder and be nonproductive. Avoid this, because a focus on ego or emotional gratification is a drought to inspiration and affection (important to creative expression) and destructive to love relationships.

Depending on the chart, it is at this time that you might take a young person under your wing who is in some way considered unacceptable. Also, if Lilith is in the fifth or elsewhere in the chart well aspected to the ruler of the fifth, your leadership ability, or the ability to take matters into your own hands, may be noticed and appreciated by others during this period.

Leisure time activities do not go well, if at all, if you are not learning, teaching, or accomplishing something during the process that is unique, unusual, or different. As Lilith has no identity with the superficial of festive occasions, parties, relaxation, and leisure, it will deny, distort, or frustrate the experience. This is also true if Lilith is square the fifth house ruler.

Children in your care, or a young person that you have to deal with, may be more rebellious now, strangely independent, or in a rather unique situation. Interest yourself in some area that they are interested in as a way to encourage communication between you or for what is preoccupying them (if they will tell you)—or just leave them alone. If you must advise, let it be to inspire their self-respect, learning, or higher interests, or use respectful and sensitive reason to connect with their essential individuality. They are feeling independent now and will not settle for anything less, as you will learn if you ignore it. Avoid any emotionalism on your part or injecting your own personality on them, or it will muddy the atmosphere and it will be as if you do not exist to them or appreciate them.

In many instances this may simply be a period when a child takes a trip, is away for some time during the period for any number of reasons, or is determined to do something different. They are expressing their will now and will not stand for any comparisons to siblings, peers, or what they did before.

In the Sixth House
In the house that Lilith magnifies for the period, awareness is always alerted to the realities behind the obvious. In the sixth it may abruptly focus your attention (or fears) on your physical wellbeing, as symptoms now can be particularly exaggerated beyond normal standards. Lilith colors the period with some preoccupation for a health matter, or the general state of your health or diet, like a nagging conscience, as if warning you to take stock of your basic living habits or to get a check-up. In all probability you will have had a checkup of one kind or another scheduled for this month.

You may be taken up with the health concerns of another, or it may be that during this period you develop greater interest in nutrition. It may that you become aware that your diet is poor or your weight out of the norm. In some cases you may continue to indulge in what you know is an unhealthy diet or sloppy personal habits. However, enjoyment of it is continually dampened because of a nagging conscience (or someone's literal nagging) that is alerting you to your foolishness. Ordinarily, you might have been able to ignore it, but it is particularly biting to you now. You might say that Lilith is relentlessly focusing an irritating reality about those things that you have been able to successfully avoid until now. Weight may suddenly jump to dangerous proportions, scaring you or causing you to appear so ungainly that out of sheer vanity you are forced to do something about it.

Because Lilith magnifies the house it influences, any health problems indicated in the natal chart for the solar year are most likely to erupt during the period that Lilith is in the sixth of a lunar return or aspecting the return's sixth or first house ruler. This is particularly so if steps have not been previously taken to correct it. You might say that it catches up with you now. The part of the body ruled by the sign Lilith occupies for the period of the return may be more sensitive, troublesome, or come under strain now. One of the exceptions to this is when Lilith is aspecting the Moon from the sixth, in which case it could be the part of the body ruled by the sign of the Moon. This need not necessarily be difficult, depending upon other factors in the chart, but simply exaggerate any unhealthy condition.

There may be a situation that causes you to put unusual stress on a part of the body, as it did for a woman attending a seminar and staying at a college dorm in hilly upstate New York. Lilith was in Aquarius square Uranus (no natal aspect between the two). Not being able to obtain any help in carrying two heavy pieces of luggage up a rather steep hill, she developed sore ankles from the strain of the climb. She had to make that trip to the dorm twice a day, which made the already weakened ankles vulnerable under her weight. She feared twisting an ankle and very nearly did coming down a flight of old stairs in the main building. As if this were not enough, the elevator in the dorm broke down one morning and she had to walk down eleven flights. She had not brought any decent walking shoes. She learned a valuable lesson about taking care of her feet, ankles, and lower legs with good supportive shoes. She could have had a very dangerous fall.

You may need to take care of health insurance or there may be a sudden problem about a payment on a claim. You may also realize health care coverage is inadequate.

Work or work habits could be successfully revamped during this period for greater efficiency, because technicalities and intricate work detail challenge the best from your mind. Imagination (creativity) is necessary in your work or if you are in a literary field. A frustration may suddenly come to your attention with or from a coworker or employee that may be almost impossible to resolve if you cannot keep personalities out of it. Concern yourself with the job for the sake of the job, seek only the most pragmatic solutions, or simply refuse to be dragged into it. Keep these relationships, as well as those with service people, strictly impersonal or you may run into a surprising outburst or unusually critical remarks from one who feels unfairly treated or unappreciated. Avoid any office intrigue during this period, as it will only spell trouble in the long run. You may temporarily work in another office or location, and have to work under strange (to you) conditions. Do not be afraid to try a different approach in your work this month.

In the Seventh House
On the positive side, Lilith's liberating action may indicate the time of the partner's vacation, a trip, creative self-renewal, or some manner in which his or her daily burdens are temporarily lifted. In any case the partner is more removed from the usual daily routine you share together. He or she is more inward or impersonal now because of preoccupation with other things. Emotionally, there is no response, or this is somehow denied.

When at home, the partner may do more reading during this time or prefer to concentrate on close detail work in a hobby or a particular interest that is more satisfying to the mind or spirit. The partner may seem to be cutting himself or herself off from the usual routine and display little patience with interruptions. The mate may change something about his or her appearance that reflects a change in attitude.

Rising above the seventh cusp, Lilith affects relationships made at this time. When negative, you may run into or be tempted into an unhealthy relationship. In this case the other party is emotionally unstable (appearances to the contrary) and the relationship should be avoided. There is something about it, that while being natural for the other, is not natural for you.

If you are counseling someone (a seventh house matter) and Lilith is in your return seventh, be particularly aware that the person has a self-insulating, emotional blindspot that can create a defensive barrier because of an inability to detach enough for impersonal evaluation. If you cannot reach the person strictly through the intellect (reason), the reaction you run into is distorted out of proportion to what you say. Resulting criticism of you is more a resentment of your intrusion into their personality than anything you may have said.

When negative, as in this case, the client seeks verification of what he or she wants to hear, rather than any ideas you may have. On the other hand, where a client is a strongly mental or creative type, a detached individual to begin with, you may have some of the most successful sessions you have ever had and do the client much good. Lilith is extreme, one way or the other.

In the Eighth House
There is compulsion to rid yourself of things or activities that have served their purpose or to eliminate associations you believe simply waste your time. It grows as the return period having Lilith in the eighth wears on. You feel a greater need for privacy, even secrecy, depending upon signs and aspects. You feel a growing sense of destiny and may become preoccupied with the occult. You may deal with one who is interested in such things. You may note an increase in your powers of observation as well as a keen awareness of being observed. Although you may be outwardly involved in your usual routines, you feel a haunting sense of displacement that you cannot seem to shake. Although aware of your daily routine, it is as if you are dealing with it now from a changing sense of direction. Something may happen that you ordinarily would feel strongly about, but now you do not; it is as though you are emotionally disconnected from the situation, as if it is a *fait accompli*. It may be at this time that Lilith in the eighth pertains to a death or rebirth (or simply a death) of a relationship with a person in a powerful position, or with an organization.

People sense a fascinating magnetism or power in you now and may consider offering you an important position or, if negative, feel strangely uncomfortable with you and write you off. You may feel intimidated by things that ordinarily you might have just overlooked. You can be more persuasive and penetrating in your observations now if you listen more and say less. Only extreme impersonality about your affairs relieves a growing tension you feel about people in your life knowing too much about you. You prefer more privacy.

This may be a period when you deal with people who remember someone who has passed away, or it may be that someone who has passed on is very much in your thoughts. Awareness of one who may be dying, or the possibility of it, enters into conversation. All of these events may also be true when return Lilith is in Scorpio or aspecting the eighth house ruler.

Taxes or joint financial matters may require serious review. A loan may be negotiated during this period. You may find yourself in a position to deeply influence one in a powerful position or give some pertinent advice on how to recycle a dying project. You may see an end to something that has served its purpose.

In the Ninth House

During this period you may find your thoughts become increasingly preoccupied with faraway places, related matters, or with or for people at a distance. Travel can be successful if the purpose is for speaking, as in the case of a lecturer; learning, as in the case of an artist; or attending an inspirational or out-of-town seminar. Ordinary pleasure trips or business travel are apt to be plagued with problems, or fall through.

Religious feelings may preoccupy your mind, because Lilith magnifies whatever is your particular God-consciousness or core of ethics. If you open yourself to inspiration at this time you will find higher interests, investigative reading, or simply taking a philosophical or spiritual view of things to be very rewarding. It is an excellent time for getting at the truth of something. Classes may have to be canceled if they are simply to enhance your earnings or prestige or to satisfy idle curiosity or time; in other words, for superficial (to Lilith) intent. Lilith has no reality on this level and, thus, being denied higher purpose, Lilith denies. This is not necessarily good or bad, but simply what I have continually observed. You may find college work seriously jeopardized if your work has been slipshod or poor all along.

Dealing with someone at or from a distance or to do with an important long distance communication, legal matter, or a person of this return house, such as an in-law, grandchild, third child, teacher, publisher, etc., may be strongly focused now. One of these people in your life may be doing something that is considerably different from what they have done before. You may receive a helpful book quite unexpectedly, or hear from other professionals in your field seeking your viewpoint or your advice.

In the Tenth House
Lilith is particularly excellent in the tenth house for those in creative or literary professions, where the intellectual or inspirational factor is so important, or where service is your first consideration. It is excellent for psychics, astrologers, or anyone in an unusual vocation, attracting unexpected appreciation or support. However, it is distorting or frustrating for those in ordinary businesses, or in areas that lack originality, vision, service, or creative growth. If in business this need not necessarily be difficult, but simply a time when you are well advised to temporarily put aside ordinary motivation for gain, and contribute more effort or something concrete for the betterment of your employees or coworkers, or for a higher grade of service and fairer deals for your customers. Lilith is supportive for anything different you might want to try. A superior may be replaced, triggering some insecurity in your job. Feelings of looking for greater job security may preoccupy your thoughts now. Just as Lilith is dark to the mundane eye (in the heavens), it is denying to mundane motivation in vocational affairs during this period. This accounts for some of the strangest happenings, attitudes, failures, upsets, or losses in the job environment; or that feeling of "What am I doing in this job?"

Where you have been naive about management or the conditions in your work, sloppy about the quality of your efforts, or overconfident about your reputation, you will find projects denied. Where you extend yourself in something you have done many times, things do not work out. In essence, Lilith is cancelling the negative in growth. If you are frustrated, then there is something shallow, naive, or selfish in your motivation for what you do or you realize that somehow you have outgrown this occupation. Extend your horizons to something more challenging, creative, or different and you will feel a surprising restoration of confidence and outlet. In the tenth, Lilith marks the period when you may discover conditions, people, or projects suddenly falling away which no longer or never did represent creative growth. Accept the new conditions for the time it gives you to set your sights on something higher in yourself in what you do.

People in authority over you are unusually sensitive now to personal inroads, even if they only suspect it. Personalities (familiarities) should be strictly avoided, or you will run up against some strange ego trips or resentment. Plans made now, unless unselfishly or creatively motivated, face future problems. Lilith here may mark the period that closes a professional or vocational area that you have been active in for some time.

In the Eleventh House
When Lilith occupies the eleventh house there may be an unusual happening with a friend or group, or there may be one whom you suddenly recognize from the past who reenters your life in a most unexpected way—someone whom you never expected to see again.

In the eleventh, Lilith may so heighten your awareness of people or crowds as to prompt you to seek a greater degree of separation from unnecessary encounters that may have mildly annoyed you before, but that now become an issue. However, if it serves some useful purpose, you are apt to go the other way and give it your all. Ordinarily, though, you would prefer to curl up with a good book instead of being with people. They leave you cold now unless you can share an interest that is mentally or creatively stimulating and can exchange ideas, share a unique experience, or do a favor for someone who is doing something different with his or her life. It might very well be for the person of the house Lilith co-rules in the return—the house that has Capricorn on the cusp. This is also a period when you could inspire friends toward goals or developing a talent or skill by believing in them or offering them advice or a challenge. There may be a tremendous assist for you, or inspiring support from a friend who believes in what you are doing and suddenly wants to help.

Inventiveness is heightened now if you allow your mind to wander to the possible, as a result of which, you might finally solve or take care of a long standing problem or a task that you have had.

There may be a prophetic dream or a sudden glimpse into the future that is very clear. Your mind is more preoccupied with the future than it is with the present, strangely feeling that the present is important only in that it is a means to that end, but not important in itself. You feel more estranged in certain groups. It is as if you unsciouly realize their nonexistence in your world of tomorrow, which you feel more a part of now than the present. Automatically, this is not spoken of because of the strangeness of it to you, and the risk you would rather not take of exposing something you feel that you do not quite understand in yourself yet. If you are the intellectual type to begin with, you probably do not speak of this because you do understand and do not feel it needs mentioning.

In the Twelfth House
Aside from whatever else occupies your attention this month, an interest (renewed or otherwise) in things occult, or the inner life, preoccupies your thoughts. You may enjoy books or studying with a group. When positive, you may feel unusually tuned in to influences around you, and more than ordinarily sensitive to your surroundings and to others. You may be more retiring during this period, or for some reason have the need to seclude yourself for a while from others, in order to accomplish something that demands all your time and attention. Take nothing for granted during this period. Be sure you hear things correctly, or ask that they be repeated. Make no assumptions. You are a bit more tuned out to others than usual and may be living more in your imagination than in reality. This is a tremendous position for imagination, but distinctly not conducive to clarity in factual data. Quite the contrary.

Your sense of illusion is magnified. On the practical side, check all facts rather than be tempted to deliberately ignore what you know is not so, or what you sense you would rather not know; in other words, don't be naive. On the emotional level this can be a period of burying your head in the sand or believing what you prefer to believe because it is easier. It is wise to be careful of this. Unless you can let go of the self-involvement or pride that creates such self-insulating blindspots when Lilith is in the twelfth, you can easily be misdirected or taken advantage of as the case may be.

Artistic or psychic sensitivity, to the extent that you have it, is sharpened. You gain much from silence or from being out in nature. For creative types the imagination is sharpened positively and great rushes of inspiration are felt.

During this period you may recognize something that revives an old environment or a way of doing something you have not done in years. It may revive old memories of a bygone time in your life.

Aspects in Return Charts
When interpreting the aspects, it is well to keep in mind that Lilith distorts the energy of a planet it contacts when one is living in the lower nature, and brings out the best of it when one is living in the higher, regardless of aspect. Although the square family of aspects strongly indicate self-defeating reactions in personal feelings and serious blindspots, it is your attitude that makes the difference one way or the other. For example, aspecting Uranus, Lilith surfaces hidden anxieties or intolerances, strange feelings of rebellion you might not have been aware of, a future orientation, and/or unpredictability. Lilith is not creating these situations as much as it is bringing them to a head as a way for you to rise above or get an intelligent perspective on them. In essence it is magnifying impersonality, separation, and/or intellectuality. This accounts for a surprising degree of intolerant feelings where there is emotional static, as well as humanitarian attitudes, unusual inventiveness, or near flashes of genius. It depends on how much you can separate yourself from personal concern for the sake of what is to be done. Lilith's stimulation simply specializes the planet's power for the return period—successfully with the impersonal, and denying or distorting it all out of proportion within the impersonal. Lilith is exaggeration anyway, so in square or opposition it is far more compulsive (or mentally or creatively stimulating if attitudes are positive) than when in trine or sextile.

If Lilith is square Pluto in the return, it is specializing its investigative or altering influence within the higher nature and distorting it in the lower. The house matters Pluto represents during that period, while denied for personal satisfaction, can be incredibly successful otherwise. Let us say that Pluto is ruling the second house in the return. During the period of time the return represents, personal security may create concern, or your self-worth may suffer. This is because the need now is to transform your values toward higher things. It may be time to let go of something that, for all practical purposes, is no longer worthy.

Consider also if no square exists natally between Lilith and Pluto, this is simply a time for some experiential growth toward higher values for yourself, and your self-sufficiency in the future. If an aspect does exist natally, the force of the square in the return is attracting the conditions the natal aspect promises for such growth. It will be more than just an experience and will somehow leave conditions altered. The idea is not to overreact. If the natal aspect is an opposition, it has to do with a relationship; if a trine, it is a buttress for the time when something or someone supportive comes along to assist your worth to grow; if a sextile, there is an opportunity; and so on. Aspecting Venus, it focuses social urges, legal matters gifts, or money. If it is to take advantage of someone's good nature, a gift may be the ugliest thing you've ever seen; but if your intentions with the person giving it have always been more or less sincere, the gift may have a touching and inspiring quality about it.

Generally, the type of aspect is not as important as the motive behind the person's action, in order to determine success or not with Lilith. Granted, the soft aspects are easier, but the hard aspects need not be impossible. It is the degree of impersonality that makes the difference. However, in dealing with the specifics for studying an aspect in the return, it is always wise to make yourself aware of how the two particular planets are natally aspected, as these characteristics are the ones primarily ingrained in the makeup and so will more greatly monitor the response. For example, the Moon trine Mars in a return chart calculated for someone having a natal semisquare of the two (the return connection reinforces the natal semisquare), the trine between them would signify supportive energy for a new public or domestic project. However, the initial frictional energy from the natal aspect (semisquare) might cause the person to misinterpret what is essentially a minor situation, due to impatience. He or she may act prematurely, or respond from an incorrect first impression to the situation that creates friction, when there need be none if a little more time had passed. When there is a square between two planets that are natally trine, the situation is more easily handled because it is not in the nature to overreact. Therefore, it represents difficulties that the individual can more readily and quickly deal with.

Keep this in mind as you interpret Lilith aspects and you will read them correctly. Also, Lilith separating from a planet indicates residual results from a previous period. Applying to an aspect, Lilith indicates one in the making where you could have more control and, of course, exact or near exact aspects create an immediate situation very near the onset of the return.

Six degrees of orb is sufficient for the planets and eight for the lights, but if a natal aspect of Lilith or the house that it tenants is being repeated in the return, consider a slightly wider orb since deeply embedded natal characteristics are surfacing.

www.ingramcontent.com/pod-product-compliance
Lightning Source LLC
Chambersburg PA
CBHW080452170426
43196CB00016B/2773